Selected Writings of the Russian Futurian

Translated by Paul Schmidt
Edited by Charlotte Douglas

THE KING OF TIME

Velimir Khlebnikov

Harvard University Press
Cambridge, Massachusetts London, England

Printed in the United States of America
10 9 8 7 6 5 4 3 2

First Harvard University Press
paperback edition, 1990.

Library of Congress Cataloging in Publication Data

Khlebnikov, Velimir, 1885–1922.
The king of time.

Includes index.
1. Khlebnikov, Velimir, 1885–1922—Translations, English. I. Schmidt, Paul, 1934– . II. Douglas, Charlotte, 1936– . III. Title.
PG3476.K485A27 1985 891.78′309 85-5560
ISBN 0-674-50515-8 (cloth)
ISBN 0-674-50516-6 (paper)

Acknowledgments

In 1980, the Dia Art Foundation commissioned a translation of the complete writings of Velimir Khlebnikov. This book represents a selection from the projected enterprise, which will be published in several volumes over the next years. A project of this kind can never be a solitary endeavor; we have a host of coworkers. Our gratitude to the directors of the Dia Art Foundation for their vision and their support of the work of translation; to our Russian colleagues, who gave encouragement and support through their publications and in personal communication—Victor Petrovich Grigoriev of the Russian Language Institute, Alexander E. Parnis, Nikolai Ivanovich Khardzhiev, and especially Khlebnikov's nephew Mai Miturich, who welcomed us and gave us access to his valuable archive. The late Professor Roman Jakobson initially encouraged us to undertake this work and allowed us to consult his personal papers. Our research could not have proceeded without the important studies of other Khlebnikovians: Henryk Baran, Barbara Lönnqvist, Vladimir Markov, and Ronald Vroon. We are fortunate in having Professor Vroon as consultant to our project; his insights into Khlebnikov are always expert and illuminating. Most of all, we thank our coworker Katherine Theodore, whose tranquillity and good humor keeps all this together, day in, day out.

A note about our work methods: as in all long-term collaborations, it is difficult after a point to separate out the individual contributions. In general we worked this way: in the case of the prose pieces, Paul Schmidt first translated the texts, and they were then carefully gone over by Charlotte Douglas, who made criticisms, corrections, and editorial comments. This process was especially pertinent for the theoretical essays, where the texts went back and forth between us many times. In the case of the poems, Schmidt takes full responsibility for the translations, although Douglas' comments were always a necessary part of the process. All the texts were read by Ronald Vroon, and his emendations are constantly reflected in the finished work.

Contents

Introduction · 1

POEMS · 11

FICTIONS · 59
Mrs. Laneen · 63
The World in Reverse · 68
Usa-Gali · 76
Nikolai · 79
K · 85
October on the Neva · 105

PROJECTS FOR THE FUTURE · 111
"Let them read on my gravestone" · 116
The Word as Such · 119
The Letter as Such · 121
!Futurian! · 123
The Trumpet of the Martians · 126
An Appeal by the Presidents of Planet Earth · 130
Ourselves and Our Buildings. Creators of Streetsteads · 133
The Head of the Universe. Time in Space · 144
To the Artists of the World · 146
On Poetry · 152
The Radio of the Future · 155
A Cliff Out of the Future · 160

EXCERPT FROM
THE TABLES OF DESTINY · *165*

ZANGEZI:
A SUPERSAGA IN TWENTY PLANES · *187*

Chronology · *239*

Indexes · *249*

Illustrations

Photograph of Velimir Khlebnikov with brother Alexander, ca. 1888 · *page xi*

Photograph of Khlebnikov in gymnasium uniform, ca. 1899 · *page xii*

Khlebnikov, drawing of bird, ca. 1900 · *page 10*

Khlebnikov, drawing of frog, ca. 1900 · *page 10*

Khlebnikov, landscape with fir trees, oil on canvas, ca. 1902–1904 · *page 12*

Photograph of Khlebnikov, 1912 · *page 60*

Vladimir Mayakovsky, drawing of Khlebnikov, 1916 · *page 110*

Khlebnikov, drawing of Vladimir Tatlin, ca. 1915 · *page 112*

Khlebnikov, architectural sketches, ca. 1919. Courtesy VEB Verlag der Kunst Dresden · *page 115*

Photograph of Khlebnikov with Sergei Esenin and Anatoly Mariengof, Kharkov, 1920 · *page 164*

Porfiry Krylov, drawing of Khlebnikov, 1922 · *page 166*

Pyotr Miturich, bathhouse at Santalovo, 1922 · *page 188*

Pyotr Miturich, Khlebnikov on his bier, 1922 · *page 236*

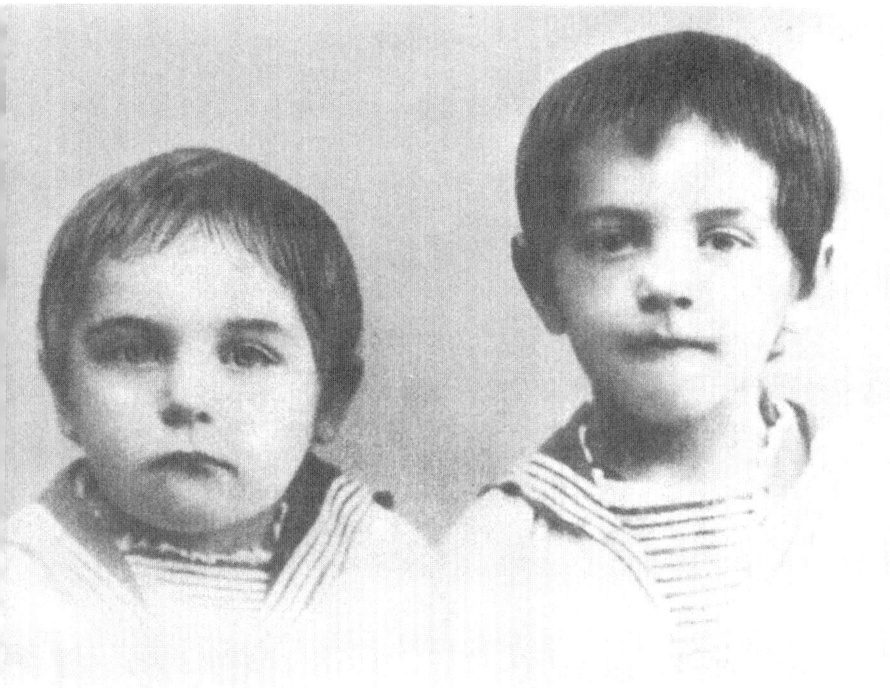

Velimir Khlebnikov (left) with brother Alexander, ca. 1888

Khlebnikov in gymnasium uniform, ca. 1899

Introduction

During the last decade, Russia has been discovering the work of one of her most remarkable poets, Velimir Khlebnikov. His name, read in English, still inspires no general recognition. Even among literate Russians for a long time his name rarely evoked more than just a few provocative texts and echoes of earlier literary judgments: "difficult," "fool," "Futurist." Now, however, as our view of Planet Earth lengthens, the scope of his work is becoming apparent and the astonishing beauty of his verbal inventions is brought into focus. Khlebnikov was an "inventor/explorer" of the early twentieth century, a master of modernism, and a verbal technician of unsurpassed brilliance. It is an appropriate sign of hope, at the present moment of global disunion, that the world beyond Russia should begin to know the work and ideas of a man who thought of himself as King of Time and President of Planet Earth.

Victor Vladimirovich Khlebnikov (later he invented the name Velimir) was born in 1885 in eastern Russia into the family of a naturalist. He attended school in Kazan and studied mathematics and science at the University there before moving, at the age of twenty-three, to the capital city of St. Petersburg. After an attempt to associate himself with a group of prominent Symbolist writers, Khlebnikov joined a more avant-garde circle of young artists and writers who were to become known as the Russian Cubo-Futurists. The group included David Burliuk, a poet, painter, and organizer, the poet Elena Guro, her husband Mikhail Matiushin, a musician and artist, the poet and theorist Alexei Kruchonykh, the artist Kazimir Malevich, and poets Vladimir Mayakovsky and Vasily Kamensky. Opposed in principle to the tasteful "literariness" of the Symbolists, the Cubo-Futurists advocated a poetics based on a common, even coarse, vocabulary and subject matter, a fastpaced line, and an emphasis on verbal material for its own sake: puns, double entendre, logical absurdities, grammatical confusions, and unrelated and incongruous images. To popularize their art in the period from about 1910 to the beginning of World War I, the Cubo-Futurists set out deliberately to shock the middle class: they organized public readings where they appeared in extravagant costumes with painted faces and radishes in their buttonholes, haranguing audience members and spilling tea in their laps; they sponsored art exhibitions and polemical debates that were the cause of continual public uproar and critical controversy. More important, perhaps, they published small books of prose and poetry, illustrated by such artists as Malevich, Mikhail Larionov, and Natalia Goncharova, who were later to become famous as early proponents of abstract art. In deliberate contrast to the luxurious and finely printed Symbolist journals, the Cubo-Futurist booklets sported burlap covers, pages made of wallpaper, and irregular punctuation and typography. Most of Khlebnikov's early poems and stories appeared in these stylistically revolutionary artists' books.

The Cubo-Futurism of these young Russian artists developed at the same time as Cubism and Futurism in Western Europe, and clearly some of their sources of inspiration were Western: the bright simplicity of Matisse's paintings, readily seen in great private collections in Moscow, had a dominant impact on Russian styles in art before 1912, and Matisse himself visited Russia in 1911 to great popular acclaim. The French Symbolist theories of René Ghil and the Unanamists also informed the Cubo-Futurist aesthetic. Still the Russian movement was not a simple borrowing from the West. While it is true that several members of the Russian avant-garde were particularly attracted to the elements of philosophical idealism in Cubism, almost all of them rejected the urban, military, and technological themes of Italian Futurism. Khlebnikov even invented the term "Futurian" to distinguish his group from the more well-known Italians. When Marinetti came to Russia early in 1914, several of the Cubo-Futurists angrily refused to acknowledge his artistic precedence. Khlebnikov in particular was furious at Marinetti's implied paternity of Cubo-Futurism and tried to disrupt one of his public lectures; he had to be thrown out of the hall where Marinetti was speaking.

For Khlebnikov, as for most of these Russian artists, a significant source of inspiration can be found in their attraction to the naive and native art of their own Slavic background. They were not impressed with the turn-of-the-century love of romanticized folklore—such as inspired the operas of Rimsky-Korsakov, for example, and the exotic renderings of local color that Diaghilev first brought to Paris. Rather, it was the crudeness and rough vitality of the living peasant past, primitive, alogical, full of rituals and taboos, that fascinated them. Vladimir Tatlin's 1911 sets for his production of the folk play *Tsar Maximilian,* for example, reproduced the coarse vigor of popular woodcuts, and Malevich and Goncharova painted subjects derived from peasant and village life. Khlebnikov and Kamensky were attracted to the primitive past of Russia, and for both poets the legendary Stenka Razin was an archetypal figure, the hero of Kamensky's novel *Stenka Razin* and a number of Khlebnikov's poems.

When Khlebnikov first began collaborating with the poet Alexei Kruchonykh, they produced crude hand-printed texts whose language was full of doggerel and humor. Their collaboration soon became more theoretical: although their ideas often differed, the two poets were responsible for a large part of the Cubo-Futurist theory that underlay the literary and artistic practice of the avant-garde. The two poets originated the idea of a suprarational, transcendental language of the future: they called it *zaum* or beyonsense. It was a language of new words based on Slavic roots and the sounds indicated by individual letters of the alphabet; Khlebnikov and Kruchonykh believed these sounds would convey emotions as well as abstract meanings forcefully and directly, without the mediation of common sense. This volume includes their two collaborative pieces from 1913, "The Word as Such" and "The Letter as Such," where they call attention to the word and letter as objects that can be manipulated in order to carry expressive meaning. This notion of Khlebnikov's, that stable units of sound material could be uncovered beneath the seemingly disorganized surface variety of language, was a vital and immediate contribution to Malevich's Suprematist style of abstract painting, as well as to the constructivist art of Vladimir Tatlin.

In December 1913, on alternate evenings with Mayakovsky's play *Tragedy*, the Cubo-Futurists staged their opera *Victory over the Sun,* with music by Matiushin, sets and costumes by Malevich, book by Kruchonykh and a prologue by Khlebnikov. Khlebnikov's part in it might have been somewhat larger, but he lost the money Matiushin had sent him to come to the early work sessions on the opera ("I went swimming and dropped my wallet in the pond," he wrote to Matiushin). *Victory over the Sun* was one of the first totally modern pieces of twentieth-century performance art. Three and a half years before Satie and Picasso's *Parade,* and in a northern city that Paris knew little about, masked performers in stylized geometric costumes danced and sang absurdly before proto-abstract backdrops. In spite of the public scandal and the adverse critical reactions it caused, the opera became a touchstone of avant-garde creativity. The Cubo-Futurists recognized the importance of its new artistic forms and defended and pursued its creative ideas.

In that exuberant company Khlebnikov may have seemed somewhat introverted. He was soft-spoken, shy, and awkward. He traveled constantly and so was often absent from the cities where these groups of artists led their extravagant lives. And yet his creative presence was crucial to them. They acknowledged the influence of his ideas and theories, and the strange appeal of his poems. When the war began and these Russian artists found themselves cut off from the rest of Europe, they intensified their creative efforts, and each of them in his own way began to further Khlebnikov's inventions and explorations.

The First World War brought on a brutal time in Russia. The country consumed all its energy and resources in the struggle to defend itself, and normal living came to an end. In 1916 Khlebnikov was drafted into the army, which he hated ("Marching, orders, it's murdering my sense of rhythm and makes me crazy"), and for the next few years he drifted in and out of military situations and across Russia in the chaos attendant upon the February and October revolutions of 1917 and the ensuing civil war. He spent the spring and summer of 1921 in northern Persia as a civilian lecturer and journalist with the Red Army, a trip that had a powerful effect on an imagination that had always been fascinated by the East. In the fall he returned with the army to Russia, to confront the widespread starvation brought on by the civil war; the poems he wrote at this time are a painful testimony to what he witnessed. And yet during this same period of want and hardship he produced most of the prophetic visions of a technological future described in the essays included in this book: visions of the architecture of the cities of the future, the vast possibilities of flight, the worldwide communications network of television. He died in 1922, weakened by malnutrition and repeated bouts of typhus and malaria, less than a year after his return from Persia. He was just thirty-six.

Khlebnikov's short life produced an extensive and multifarious body of work. All attempts to classify him as a member of this or that school or trend—as a Utopian or an anarchizer, even as a Cubo-Futurist—derive from a consideration of part of his work only. Taken as a whole, his work explores a unique and much broader terrain. In addition to poems and plays, stories and essays, he wrote political and artistic manifestoes, essays on history, architecture, and social problems, literary theory, and journalistic pieces on current events. His passion for internationalism in politics and the arts prompted him to invent an organization called the Presidents of Planet Earth. This he envisioned as a world government of creative scientists, writers, and thinkers, dedicated to counteracting all the social evils fostered by political states.

Fundamental to the entire range of Khlebnikov's work was a holistic vision of nature; his efforts were attempts to understand humanity's place within it. To that end, much of his life was devoted to searching for the "Laws of Time," to working out the fundamental equations that he believed govern natural and historical events. For him the world was composed of primary oscillating forces whose mathematical properties were the concrete expression of the nature of the universe and everything within it. The "law of the see-saw," as Khlebnikov referred to these cosmic equations, was a powerful unifying mechanism that he understood to connect such disparate phenomena as the sounds of words, an individual's changes of mood, luck and personal events, and the rise and fall of great nations. It is tempting to consider these explorations as an intellectual aberration, but we would be wrong to do so. The history of science labors under a burden shared by no other branch of history: it is judged retrospectively through the highly selective lens of our current conception of truth and fiction. Science, progressing through the process of selection and rejection, affords us answers to our questions about the universe, but we must be careful not to confuse those answers with the process of finding them. The process of discovery—the way of the "inventor/explorer"—may be significant in its own right. Khlebnikov's ideas about the vibratory nature of the universe, for example, can be related to tantric cosmic theory and to quantum mechanics, a fact of particular interest for historians of modern ideas. Khlebnikov believed that scientists, poets, and artists are all engaged in the same enterprise—the search for a successful way to conceive of nature. At the end of his life he believed he had indeed found a general law that held true for many different types of phenomena, and on the basis of this discovery he even felt able to make general predictions about the nature of future events. And he saw this not as limiting our notion of human possibilities, but rather as liberating us from the blindness of fate. The scientific validity of his theories as judged from our point of view today is of less consequence than their effect on his work then, and their importance for our understanding of it now.

It is above all the extraordinary excellence of his poetry that justifies Khlebnikov and his endeavors. He ranks with Mallarmé, Joyce, Pound, and Stein among the great innovators of literary modernism. His experiments broke the hold of traditional verse patterns in Russian poetry. He worked with irregularities, unequal line lengths, meters that varied from line to line in a single poem, variable stanza length, irregular rhyme patterns. He made use of patterns and tropes from folklore and from chants, incantations and shamanistic language. And he managed to create an entire poetics in that area of language the Anglo-Saxon tradition tends to belittle as "play"—neologisms, palindromes, riddles, puns.

This kind of writing poses a real challenge to the translator of Khlebnikov, who must become an "inventor/explorer" in his own turn. He must try to work upon American English the same sorts of transformations that Khlebnikov works upon Russian. This act of language must begin in much the same way an actor prepares, in a similar language act, to create a character on stage. The translator must internalize as much as he can the same influences that worked upon his author; he must read the same books, visit the places he lived, imagine the noise and smell of his time, and then try to seek out or create simulacra in his own time, the time and space of a different culture and a different language. This approach has the advantage of seeing translation as process, as a cultural and temporal response to the original text, and it helps to avoid concentrating on the text of the translation as somehow an imitation of the original, which it cannot be. It is a new text, a product of response in its own time and place.

Formal poetic problems must be dealt with individually in the task of translating Khlebnikov, so the customary all-embracing apologies for translation—"I have aimed at lexical fidelity," or "I have kept the rhyme scheme of the original," or "This is a plain word-for-word translation, faithful to the sense"—are not possible here. No one rule seems suitable for such a vast and shifting terrain of language. Consider the matter of neologisms, for example. Khlebnikov's forms are based on the most varied patterns of word formation, and similar patterns can often be found in English. But frequently the semantic field the neologism refers to seems of less importance than our perception of the *act* of neologizing. The semantic field is inevitably vague: it is the process of neologizing that is brought into sharp focus. Translation proceeds here somewhat on the model of Venn diagrams. The translator is forced to explore, to invent a structure that will call attention to itself while retaining a relevant semantic overlap with the Russian model.

For the American translator, there is one fortunate correspondence to be found at the very beginnings of Khlebnikov's creativity: the undoubted influence upon him of Walt Whitman. Whitman's long, variable line was a model for the young Khlebnikov; "O Garden of Animals," in this volume, shows it clearly. This line resounds strongly in Russian against the four-beat iambic rhythms of his other early poems, which were so much a part of the Russian Pushkinian heritage. The echo of Whitman's American language, then, is a familiar landfall for the translator on his voyage of exploration.

A fundamental source for Khlebnikov's material is the great dictionary of Vladimir Dahl, a mine of lore on the Russian language, on dialect forms, on folk speech and customs. Over and over we find Khlebnikov using it to explore the substrata of Russian speech, reading back into the past of his language, where forms gradually recede into a magic distance. Every entry in Dahl will send the translator of Khlebnikov to the *Oxford English Dictionary,* to Webster, to Partridge, to Bartlett. The *O.E.D.* in particular helps us to reach backward into English toward those sounds that constitute the "universal truths passing before the predawn of our soul" that Khlebnikov describes in his essay "On Poetry." It is a magic apparent on the dictionary page, for we trace the evolution of a word through time. We watch it ask and answer the riddle of itself: what is unchanging in the constantly changing forms of a given word?

Consider for instance the poem "Incantation by Laughter." Khlebnikov takes the Russian word for laughter, *smekh,* and creates a chant of new words based on it, using the Russian rules of allowable word formation. American English is much poorer in such rules than Russian, and the word "laugh" also suffers a hopelessly outdated spelling, which helps to weaken any sound patterns we might try to make. So our translation offers neologisms excavated from the history of the word "laugh" in the *O.E.D.,* in an attempt to respond to the richness and complexity of the Russian text—with, frankly, something funny enough to laugh at. And this process is completely in accord with Khlebnikov's intentions.

The use of neologisms and word games can be off-putting to the reader of English, who feels it detracts from the high seriousness poetry must possess. Yet such an attitude ignores the essential nature of all poetry as word play. The seriousness of Khlebnikov's intentions in any case helps to defend him from any charge of frivolity or obscurantism.

What astonishes us is to discover that in Khlebnikov the conventional impulse to poetry—the attempt to identify the self through poetic expression—gave way early to an attempt to identify the universe through poetry, to locate it and mark its coordinates in the sounds of language themselves, and in their vibrations to make resound these "strings" that comprise the universe and hold it together. This passionate belief in the sovereignty of a lawful nature gave Khlebnikov a great intellectual freedom in the pursuit of its boundless variety, in poetry and in the various languages he devised for poetry. It removed the constraints of common forms and opened words to the wide prospects enjoyed by natural objects, while making them subject to the deep scrutiny of analytical dissection. Khlebnikov was thus able to proceed to the work of the poet with the methodological precision of the scientist and to partake of the passion of both.

To tune mankind into harmony with the universe—that was Khlebnikov's vocation. He wanted to make Planet Earth fit for the future, to free it from the deadly gravitational pull of everyday lying and pretense, from the tyranny of petty human instincts and the slow death of comfort and complacency. He wanted to transform the World through the Word. He deserved the title his friends conferred on him: Velimir the First, King of Time.

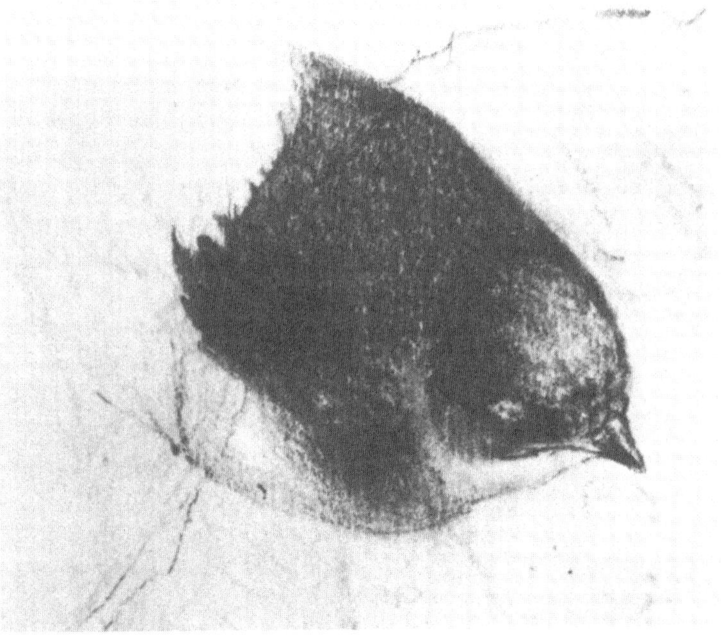

Khlebnikov, drawing of bird, ca. 1900

Khlebnikov, drawing of frog, ca. 1900

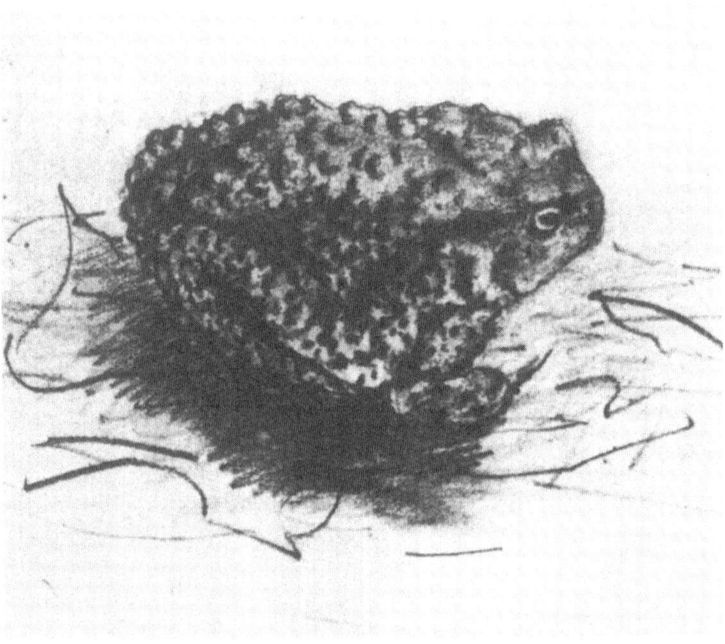

Poems

Khlebnikov, landscape with fir trees, oil on canvas, ca. 1902–1904

The poems in this section are of varied style and inspiration, as well as from different periods of Khlebnikov's creative life, but they share certain traits that are characteristic of his approach to poetry. Khlebnikov creates poems by playing with the relationship between the morphological and phonological structures of language and meaning: he makes frequent use of forms that tend to produce maximum ambiguity, such as neologisms, homonyms, puns, and nonsense. The structure of a word could be examined, Khlebnikov found, and its latent meanings laid bare; new words could be created on the models of existing ones. Much of Khlebnikov's writing, therefore, has to do with the texture of language, with poetry as made words. *His puns and neologisms are attempts to lay bare the meanings that may be hidden in the worn-out language of every day.*

Khlebnikov was convinced of the magic power of words. In the story "K" he writes: "I believe that before a major war the word pugovitsa *[button] has an especially frightening meaning, since the war—even though as yet undreamed of—lurks in that word like a conspirator, a harbinger lark, because the root of the word is related to* pugat' *[to frighten]." Now in fact the two words are not related historically, but that is precisely the point. This kind of derivation, which linguists refer to as folk etymology, was for Khlebnikov the point of entry into the hidden net of coincidences and poetic correspondences that Baudelaire first wrote of, but that for Khlebnikov are more systematic and profound. For him they reveal the workings of destiny because they point the way to the future. Just as magic words are intended to bring about a desired future, so these unexpected glimpses of "magic" patterns hidden beneath the ordinary surface of language can offer us a vision of the world to come. In a preface written in* 1919, *Khlebnikov comments that "little things are significant when they mark the start of the future . . . Whenever I saw old lines of writing grow dim and their hidden content become the present day, then I understood. The future is creation's homeland, and from it blows the word-god's wind." We touch here upon the profoundest function of poetry. Familiar language suddenly opens up, and in it something unexpected is revealed. The unexpected is always the future; it appears to us at the edges of meaning, in a moment of illumination that is simultaneously a denial of the ordinary rational use of language. Words refuse to be ideas, part of the world of human reason, which is always the world of the present. They open up the unknown, the unnamed—the world of the future. This is Khlebnikov's great perception. He is able to take a word by itself as a palpable living thing and, by working with it, make it yield new forms and new meanings.*

The problem of dating Khlebnikov's poems is an extremely complicated one. With the exception of some late poems in the notebooks, few poems are dated in manuscript. Most of the early work exists only in collections that were often printed several years after the poems were written. Khlebnikov was in the habit of revising early texts and incorporating them into longer texts that he called supersagas—such as Zangezi*—and this makes it difficult to establish any fixed date of composition. The poems that follow are grouped thematically, but the groupings have a rough chronological order.*

Khlebnikov enrolled at the University of Kazan in 1903, and it was during the next six years, in Kazan and then in Petersburg, that he began to write his first serious poetry. At this time Khlebnikov became an eager reader of the Symbolist journal Libra, *and the Symbolist mood is apparent in these poems, most of them probably written in 1908–1909; they have some of the same resonances as the early Yeats. Many of the images here recall too the birds he had pursued so attentively during an ornithological expedition to the Urals in the spring of 1905. These images finally coalesce in his first major poem, "O Garden of Animals!", a homage to Walt Whitman and a work Khlebnikov hoped would appear in a new Symbolist journal,* Apollo. *The poem was rejected by the editors, however, and Khlebnikov turned to a more congenial group of writers and artists who happily published his poem. He called them Futurians.*

Here I praise the brutal flight
Of the wings that carried me into distances,
To Freedom's signifying blue dimension
Domed by the sun with rings of light,
High, high, to that absolute height
Where the white stork of poetry sings eternally.

Languor-wing lying in the middle of fable,
Chained by your enchanting charms,
Tangled in nets of golden wool
I will die here in your arms.

The freezing weather of debauchery
Has killed the languor-wing of dawn.
The innocent idlescent dies
And the firelings bear his pall.

Came a rush of whistling,
All the birds deserted the sky.
Like rustling leaves
They would not fly.

And like a giant wing above me
I watched the swan-storm grow.
The cloud was some enormous bird
That trailed twilight on the place below.

Mysterious feathers in shadows
Drift beyond the wing's wide arc.
I fled the science of hypocrisy
And hurried headlong into the dark.

Crawling crying craven
Stains the twilight sky
Falling where the raven
Turns the why-light of his eye.

Snowfellow, tallfellow, bright beacon,
What has become of your mother?
Snowfellow, tallfellow, bright beacon,
What have they done with your mother?

Where the winking waxwings whistle
In the shadows of the cedars,
Where the branches shake and shiver
The mockingbird minutes fly away;

In the shadows of the cedars
A flock of flickers flutter,
Where the branches shake and shiver
The swallows turn to seasons
As they fly away.

The streams of time
On stone dreams,
The rush of streams
On time's stones.
Rustling sedge
At the lake's edge—
Reverent hush,
Reverberant rush.

You are my song, my dark blue dream
Of doves, of winter's drowsy drone,
And sleighs that slow and golden go
Through gray blue shadows on the snow.

O Garden of Animals!

Where iron bars seem like a father who stops a bloody fight to remind his sons they are brothers.

Where eagles perch like eternity, crowned by a day without an evening.

Where a swan is like winter all over, but its beak is like autumn leaves.

Where deer are startled again and again, beneath their branching stone.

Where a clean-shaven soldier throws dirt at a tiger, all because the tiger is greater.

Where a peacock drops its tail, and it looks like Siberia seen from the height of a rock on a day of early frost, when the golden forest fire of leaf-fall enamels the green and the mottled blue of pine groves, when over it all move shadows of racing clouds, and the rock itself seems like the body of a bird.

Where fishwingers sit comically grooming each other, and display the touching compassion of Old World Landowners.

Where man and dog are strangely joined, in a baboon.

Where a camel knows the essence of Buddhism, and suppresses a Chinese smile.

Where a snow-white beard surrounds the face of a tiger, surrounds its venerable Moslem eyes, and we honor the first Mohammedan and drink in the beauty of Islam.

Where a small bird drags behind itself a golden flattering sunset, to which it has learned to pray.

Where lions get up and glance with weary faces at the sky.

Where at last we grow ashamed of ourselves, and begin to think we are older, more worn than we once imagined.

Where elephants sway like mountains during an earthquake, and stick out their trunks for handouts from a small boy, saying "Feed me! Feed me!", echoing that ancient refrain. And they wheeze like pinetrees in autumn, and move their wise eyes and their undulating ears.

Where the polar bear hunts like an osprey, tracking his nonexistent prey.

Where we watch in a seal the torments of a sinner, as it cuts the water and wails its unrelenting wail.

Where the beasts have learned to sleep while we gawk.

Where the bat hangs sleeping, and its capsized body resembles a Russian's heart.

Where a sable displays two tiny ears, like a pair of nights in springtime.

Where I search for new rhythms, whose beats are animals and men.

Where the animals in their cages glow, as meaning glows in language.

O Garden of Animals!

The magic possibilities of language are constantly alive for Khlebnikov. He is always conscious of the wonders that are revealed in permutations in the form *of words. Puns, palindromes, word derivations, above all the creation of new words: these are fields of experimentation for him, and the experiments pass into his poems. The most famous is "Incantation by Laughter," permutations of the word* laugh *into a weird scenario full of prehistoric chortles.*

Beyond purely linguistic transformation, Khlebnikov works with many of the patterns of folk poetry. One frequent presence in his writing is the old Russian folk device of the riddle: the "enormous arboreal monster," for instance, is a lascivious garden swing, hung from the branch of a tall tree. And other poems are full of wonders: flute-playing tigers, peripatetic frogs, singing bones, the transformation of the stricken deer into the conquering lion.

This sense of the vitality of the natural world is part of Khlebnikov's heritage from Russian folklore. The magical inhabitants of the Slavic forest—the rusalka, *the* leshy, *the* vila *(river mermaid, goblin, forest enchantress)—all populate his poetry and his imagination. Khlebnikov's earliest attempts at poetry were rooted in the revival of the old Slavic tradition that was a side branch of Russian Symbolism: attractive experiments with folk languages, folk patterns even, poems as reflections of the intricate embroideries and wood carvings of peasant culture. These are the same influences that are reflected in the other arts, in Stravinsky's* Sacre du printemps *and* Les Noces *and in Goncharova's designs for Diaghilev.*

The poems that follow were most probably written between 1910 and 1915, though a few of them were published later.

Incantation by Laughter

Hlahla! Uthlofan, lauflings!
Hlahla! Ufhlofan, lauflings!
Who lawghen with lafe, who hlaehen lewchly,
Hlahla! Ufhlofan hlouly!
Hlahla! Hloufish lauflings lafe uf beloght lauchalorum!
Hlahla! Loufenish lauflings lafe, hlohan utlaufly!
Lawfen, lawfen,
Hloh, hlouh, hlou! luifekin, luifekin,
Hlofeningum, hlofeningum.
Hlahla! Uthlofan, lauflings!
Hlahla! Ufhlofan, lauflings!

We chant and enchant,
Oh charming enchantment!
No raving, no ranting,
No canting enchantment!
This ranting enchantress
Has cast her enchantment—
We see what her chant meant!
Here rant! There cant!
You charming enchanter,
Cast out her enchantment,
Uncast it, uncant it,
Discast it, discant it,
Descant: Decant! Recant!
He can't. She can't.
Why can't she recant?
Why can't he uncant?
Ranting chanting,
No recanting.
Discant, descant.

Enormous arboreal monster, horrid
Height with rump of shocking size,
Grips a girl who fetched a pail of water,
Rolling at him her cajoling eyes.
Diddled for a moment, she's an apple
In the branches of his shaggy arms.
Enormous monster—rather awful
Really—lolls and laps. Life has its charms.

I saw a Tiger, he crouched by a wood
And filled a bamboo flute with his sighs;
His ferine forces contracted in waves,
And mocking fires burned in his eyes.
Beside him an elegant maid discoursed
With an elegant tilt to her head:
"Tigers and lions, as everyone knows,
Cannot carry a tune," she said.

Who wants to hear a story
About a little lady who lived very grand,
Oh not a big-time lady really
Just a sort of fat froggie:
She was short and she waddled and she wore a dress,
And had lots of significant friendships
With pinetrees, all of them princes.
She goes visiting in springtime
And you know which way she paddles
By the bright reflecting puddles in her wake—
That silly little lady of the lake.

A greeny goblin grabbles in the forest—
A wood-willy, slurping his mouth organ—
Where a clump of aspens quivers
And benifolent spruces cascade.

A smear of pungent forest honey
Licky on the tongue-tip of daylight;
Oh! his grasping arms were icy:
I was completely taken in.

I couldn't stand his eyes' unblinking
Point-blank confrontation—
His look, full of pleading promises,
The icicle anguish in his eyes.

Hay-rake fingers crabbing at me
From a shaking flurry of flax;
He had dark blue sighters
And a body all mush-flesh and flow.

I had missed a turn or two, tearing
Along in a juventy frenzy. Slying,
The wood-wart winked and jostled
Me: "Which way where? And why?"

The Tangled Wood

The tangled wood was full of sound,
The forest screamed, the forest groaned
With fear
To see the spear-man beast his spear.

Why does hart's horn hang heavy with
Hazard, the moving mark of love?
Arrow's flying glitter hits a haunch,
And reckons right. Now beast is broken

To his knees, beaten to the ground.
His eyes look deep at death.
The horses clatter, snort and chatter:
"We bring the Tall Ones. Useless to run."

Useless only your exquisite motion,
Your almost feminine face. No action
Can save you. You fly from rack and ruin,
And searching spear-man follows fast.

Panting horses always closer,
Branching antlers always lower,
Twangling bowstrings over and over,
Nor hart nor help, from hurt and hazard.

But he rears abruptly, bristles, roars—
And shows a lion's cruel claws.
With lazy ease he touches, teases—
Teaches the trick of terror.

Acquiescent and still,
They fall to fill their graves.
He rises rampant. Regal
Regard. Observing the bodies of slaughtered slaves.

Rue: A Fable

You know the herb they use for doses;
It grows at the edge of filthy places.
This is a tale of ancient princes:
Russia fought the Mongols here
In the heavy days of a younger year.
With a rough sack of sour complaints
New Year came to take his place,
With all his horde of helpmates hustling
After, joking, jostling, whistling
Lewdly into their country pipes
And puffing out their piggy cheeks.
But that same land no longer laughs
Since the swan-song sounded overhead,
And the bones, the bones—"Rue," they cry

Beneath their shroud of spring-green rye.
And the bones, they wail forevermore:
"We will always remember war."

Black king dance out front of the crowd,
And witch-doctors batter the tom-tom.
Big black women laugh bawdy and loud,
Pelele stain their mouth, and burn.
The dirty kettle bubble,
Some bird bones, and a child.
Our Elder Father Helper Sun
He hurt us unaware.
Seven times the light go by
Seven times to earth from sun.
We look and see the dark turn cold.
We look and we see Requiem.
Black king dance out front of the crowd,
And witch-doctors batter the tom-tom.

Rutting elephants, battering ivory tusks
That seemed white stone
Beneath an artist's hand.
Stags in rut, with antlers intertwined:
They seemed embraced in ancient intercourse,
In tugging ardors and adulteries.
Rivers hurled themselves into the sea:
Seemed? The hand of one strangled the neck of another.

Glitter-letter wing-winker,
Gossamer grasshopper
Packs his belly-basket
With water-meadow grass.
Ping, ping, ping! throstle-whistle

Sing-song.
Swan-wing wonder!
Nightlessness! Brightness!

The sayings and sallies of spring
Poke through the pages of winter's volumes,
And somebody blue-eyed reads
The scribblings of frost-frazzled nature.

A little gold ball flies through the net
Of a budding poplar's branches.
These days the golden coltsfoot moves
Like a huddle of golden turtles.

Alive with glad tidings,
A spring-green Koran,
My poplar up early expects
Emissaries of dawn.
Out to snare the sun-fish
In the blue pond overhead,
It tosses its meshes
And neatly nets the bellow of bulls,
A lazy-pacing thunderhead
And the bright fragrance of a summer storm.
My poplar-angler,
Natural tower,
You cast your green meshes
High and wide from your trunk
And there! the god of springtime
Gapes, a sun-fish astonished
In the boat-bottom
Of every glistening leaf.
Green mouth greets high heaven,
Eats it up! Snare for sun-gods,
My high-flying Poplar

With horn-roar and wind-blow
Unleashes a wallop
That washes the meadow
In a wave of blue vodka.

A bunch of yellow buttercups.
Lightning's evil eye.
A woman drops a pale flower, walks on by.
And soon the eyes of windows bang
Beneath the hurly-burly hanging over our heads.
The yellow-backed book gets soaking wet.
The rumbling clouds are blue and black.
In the kingdom of hearing two castles collapse
And out jumps that powerful female cat,
The thunderstorm! . . . who glowers
At the drooping flowers.

Most of the poems in the following group were published between 1914 and 1916. Here, Khlebnikov's cosmic vision begins to grow. The correspondences between elements of the natural world suddenly expand to include abstract phenomena like numbers and the movement of the stars and planets; history echoes in sounds drifting on the water; the names of the great creators of human culture resound in the wind and rain. The folkloric patterns in Khlebnikov blend with his studies in the sciences; the magical, pagan, Slavic forest culture and the abstract conception of mathematics fuse metaphorically:

> *I see right through you, Numbers.*
> *I see you in the skins of animals,*
> *coolly propped against uprooted oaks.*

In a similar way the legendary city of Kitezh in The Tables of Destiny *rises magically from the bottom of a lake and transforms itself into a long equation whose powers and superscripts rise like crenellated towers and glitter, reflected in the water.*

Khlebnikov seems to have heard within himself not just one voice but hundreds, and was able to make out beneath their clamor the pure sounds of language forming themselves into patterns, resonating with the "sounding string of humanity." Khlebnikov was searching for the voice of Time itself, sounding in language.

Nations, faces, ages pass,
Pass as in a dream,
An ever-flowing stream.
In Nature's shifting glimmer-glass
Stars are nets, we their haul,
Gods are shadows on a wall.

The law of the see-saw argues
That your shoes will be loose or tight,
That the hours will be day or night,
And the ruler of earth the rhinoceros
Or us.

When horses die, they sigh
When grasses die, they shrivel
When suns die, they flare and expire
When people die, they sing songs.

Numbers

I see right through you, Numbers.
I see you in the skins of animals,
coolly propped against uprooted oaks.

You offer us a gift—unity between the snakey movement
of the backbone of the universe and the Dipper dancing
overhead. You help us to see centuries as a flash
of laughing teeth. See my wisdom-widened eyes.

Recognize   what I   will be
when its dividend is one.

Water eats at the rippling
Roots, flows still near the shadowy trees.
The wind wavers at odd
Or even. Nets hang still by the weir.

Perspiration blurs the hazy air.
In a place that had never heard of grief
A brooding sun-burnt boy grew up.
A girl grew up beside him.

Night-time reeds on the bank shiver
And weeds in the water tremble,
And some tall, white-faced figure
Stands near the trees, indistinguishable.

Wind whose
Song, wound
Whose wrong?
Sweat of sword
To turn to word
(I'm dead, I'm dead)
Staining arms in sanguine streams.
I renew, eye
You, know you.
Brave new.

The Song of One Come to Confusion

I saw a black branch, pine needles
On a canvas of stones;
Her hand, I thought, thin as bones—
It knocks at my very vitals.

So soon? So strange, now, to stand
Beside you in the evening, a skeleton;

To stretch out a long thin hand
And conjure my constellation into your room.

These tenuous Japanese shadows,
These murmuring Indian maidens,
Nothing sounds so mournful
As words at this last supper.
Death—but first life flashes past
Again: unknown, unlike, immediate.
This rule is the only rhythm
For the dance of death and attainment.

People in love
Making long looks, long sighs.
Beasts in love
Dregs in their eyes
Choking on bits of foam.
Suns in love
Covering night with a weft of earth
Dancing to meet, to mate.
Gods in love, forming the trembling universe
Into verse,
Like Pushkin his passion
For Volkonsky's maid.

Dostoeskimo snowstorms!
Pushkincandescence of noon!
Night resembles Tiutchev,
Filling the unfathomable full of the unknown.

I see them—Crab, Ram, Bull,
And all the world is only shell
Whose pearl and opalescence
Is my impotence.
A knock, a chirr, container of whistle and rustle,
And I realize then that waves and thoughts are kin.
Here, there, in milky ways, women rise
Through darkness drunk on drowsy prose.
On such a night, no grave is grim . . .
And evening women, evening wine
Become a single diadem
Whose baby boy I am.

Night's color breeding darker blues
Drifts over everything we love,
And one called out, the sound of it oppressive,
Full of the anguish of evening.
A moment once, when golden light,
Three stars, flamed in boats on the water,
And when a lonely juniper brushes
Its branches over a gravestone.
A moment once, when giants bound
Scarlet turbans on their heads,
And the wayward surge of the sea-wind,
Wonderful, never knowing why.
A moment once, when fishermen's voices
Echoed the words of Odysseus,
And beyond the swell in the distance
An upward wing, above the sea-wave hovering.

Genghiskhan me, you midnight plantation!
Dark blue birch trees, sound in my ear!
Zarathuse me, twilight horizons!
Mozarticulate me, dark blue sky!
Goya, gloaming, glooming!

Rops, you midnight clouds!
But the storm of smiles vanishes
In cackling and the shock of claws
And leaves me to outface the hangman,
To brave the stillness of the night.
I summoned up you barefaced insolents,
From rivers made the drowned girls rise,
Their flowering cry—rosemary, remembrance—
Reverberant in the sails of night.
Again earth's axis splashes round,
Brings on the overwhelming evening.
I dreamed I saw a salmon-girl
Beneath a midnight waterfall.
Let storm-drenched pines make Mamai-monsters
Beneath the Batu-beating clouds:
Words come on, like Cain to silences,
And all this sacred stillness dies.
And to stone entertainment with heavy foot-fall
Comes heaven-blue Hasdrubal, henchmen and all.

One of the keys to understanding any poem is its use of personal pronouns—they establish a modal center for the poem, its "signature," just as a piece of music is written in a key signature. We generally look first to the pronoun "I," the lyric subject, for an understanding of any poet's vision of himself. Khlebnikov writes often in an epic or dramatic style that avoids or detaches the pronoun "I," but in a number of his poems it becomes forthright and direct. We cannot call them confessional, and yet in them we read Khlebnikov's own experiences told simply, unmitigated by excessive verbal play. The matter of the poems that follow is the two concerns most central to any poet: his sense of himself as a poet, a visionary, and of himself as a man in love. These poems were probably written between 1914 and 1921.

The King is out of luck,
The King is under lock
    and key.
Infantry Regiment Ninety-Three
Will be the death of the child in me.

[On a postcard to a friend,
just after he was drafted, April 1916]

The naked stag-horn rising in the woods
May seem a dead tree.
When a heart is laid bone-bare in words
They scream: he's mad.

When I was young I went alone
Into the dead of night;
My hair was thick
And touched the ground.
Night was everywhere
And oh it was lonely,
Wanting friends
And wanting a self.
I set my hair on fire,
Threw the bits in a ring around me;
I burned my fields and trees
And things felt better.
Arson in Khlebnikov acres!
Burning ego flickered in the dark.
Now I depart
With flaming hair
As WE,
Not I.
Go, uncompromising Viking!
Uphold your law, and honor.

Refusal

I would rather
Watch stars
Than sign a death warrant.
I would rather
Hear flowers murmur
("It's him!")
When I'm out in the garden
Than see a gun
Shoot down a man
Who wants to shoot me down.
Which is why I would never
Be a governor.
Ever.

I'm going out again today
Into life, into the marketplace,
To lead a regiment of songs
Against the roaring, wheeling-dealing world.

Po People

A bird who strives to rise higher
Flies into the blue.
A lady who strives to rise higher
Wears a high-heeled shoe.
When I don't have any shoes
I go to the market and buy some.
Someone who's missing a nose
Can go get a false one.
When a nation discovers it has no soul,
It can go to the neighbors
And buy one! Sold!
. . . And un-souled!

Russia and Me

Russia has granted freedom to thousands and thousands.
It was really a terrific thing to do,
People will never forget it.
But what I did was take off my shirt
And all those shiny skyscrapers the strands of my hair,
Every pore
In the city of my body
Broke out their banners and flags.
All the citizens, all the men and women
Of the Government of ME,
Rushed to the windows of my thousand-windowed hair,
All those Igors and Olgas
And nobody told them to do it,
They were ecstatic at the sunshine

And peeked through my skin.
The Bastille of my shirt has fallen!
And all I did was take it off.
I have granted sunshine to the people of ME!
I stood on a beach with no clothes on,
That's how I gave freedom to my people
And suntans to the masses.

The fault is yours, you gods—
You made us mortal,
And for that we let fly at you
The poisoned arrows of our sadness.
The bow is ours.

Unbending as a Boris Godunov boyarina,
You sailed on past today, swan on a lake,
And I'd been expecting as much, I suppose.
I hadn't read daybreak's letter over.
But oh, remember? Yesterday you were a mermaid,
A real rusalka, your arms a paddle wheel
Splashing away, a rusalka's recreation,
And you set some shepherds squabbling with their flocks;
They all came running, gaping at the sight,
Then backed away and yelled at you "Rusalka!"
—A bad example for local girls
Doomed to distaffs and to homespun cloth.
But oh, remember? You were really divine,
The goddess of the place, all-knowing and passionate,
Your braids like evening doves descending
To perch on your suntanned shoulders.
It really was you! You sat in the wheatfield
And played on the midnight strands of your braids.
It really was you! To make yourself beautiful
You rubbed your body with honey, enchanting the bees.
You scrutinized my somewhat frazzled forehead
And wearily told me "tell me more"—

The dictionary-history of my early sweethearts—
As we sat together on new-mown hay.
Here was no "yes" nor will be "but";
Here "was" is forgotten, and "will be," no one knows;
Here the Dove descends on your shoulders at teatime
And Our Lady lays her washing out in rows.

Babylove, don't your eyes ever get tired
Of being so wide and beautiful?
I want you to call me little brother—will you?
If you do I swear by my own blue eyes
I'll hold up the flower of your life and protect it.
You and I are alike, I fell from the sky
Just like you, and the world keeps causing me grief.
I wasn't what they wanted, never have been,
I'm unfriendly
And no one can love me.
Let's be brother and sister. You want to?
We're both of us free, and the earth is free,
We won't be afraid of their laws, they can't hurt us,
We'll make our own laws
And model the clay of our own behavior.
You're my flower of blue, you are beautiful,
I know that, and everything's tender and sudden
When you talk about summer and sunshine
And your eyes grow wide when you do it.
I've been doubtful of everything all my life
But now I believe, instantly and forever:
A trail through Time has been blazed before us,
And no one can ever obscure it.
Let's avoid a lot of useless words.
I'll be your long-haired priest
And just say Mass.
I'll drink the blue waters of purity
And names will never hurt us.

[September 13, 1921]

Once more, once more
I am
Your star.
Woe to the sailor with level
And compass
Whose angle is false.
He will wreck on rocks
And hidden shoals.
Woe to you without love
Or compassion
Who angled me false.
You will wreck on rocks
And the rocks will laugh
at you
the way you did
at me.

In 1921, in connection with his activities as a civilian publicist with the military on the southern front, Khlebnikov suddenly got the chance to go to Persia as a journalist and lecturer with the Red Army. In mid-April he sailed for Enzeli, ecstatic at the sun and sea, and the opportunity finally to be in the East he had felt a part of for so long. He stayed for a time as a tutor in the house of a Talysh Khan and explored coastal and inland villages, tanned and long-haired, dressed in native robes, living on handouts. "I told the Persians," he wrote, "that I was a Russian prophet."

All the poems that relate to his sojourn in Persia are full of excitement and events: the thrill of travel, exotic landscapes, the turmoil of revolution—Khlebnikov mentions the exploits of his friend, the revolutionary sailor Boris Samorodov—possible experiments with drugs. But above all, his time in Persia seems to have confirmed his sense of vocation. His poem "Night in Persia," with its reference to the Mekhdi (Mahdi), the Islamic messiah, is filled, like Pushkin's "Prophet," with wonder at the divine visitation that turns a poet into a spokesman for the ineffable.

The pull of Asia was very strong in Khlebnikov, partly as a result of his upbringing near the Caspian and partly as a corrective for what he considered the excessive Western European influence on Russian culture—an attitude documented in manifestos like "!Futurian!" But even more important is Khlebnikov's vision of the land mass of Asia as the center of the world of the Future, when Slavic culture would join with the cultures of Islam, Hinduism, and Buddhism to form an unshakable foundation for a regenerated planet.

The smell of night, and stars
We seemed about to breathe, wildly
Where water lay everywhere
And what we said went sliding
Into the surf.

A figure passes, you, and on your head
A green turban of dried grass—
I recognize my teacher, your face
Burned bonfire black.

And another approaches,
Exhausted as all Asia. See?
He holds in his hand
A small red flower.

Asia, I have made you my obsession.
As maidens touch their brows, I grasp at thunderclouds;
I grasp your nighttime conversation
as I would reach for tender vibrant shoulders.
Where is he who prophesied a day of unconstrained caresses?
If only Asia's hair in dark blue streams
would flood my knees, envelop me,
and a maiden whisper secret reprehensions,
and then in silent rapture sob
and with her braid-ends brush away her tears.
She has loved! Yes, and suffered! She is
the dark soul of the universe!
Then would feelings once more flood my heart
and kindle there the jangling of catastrophe,
of Mokhavir, Zoroaster, Savadzhi,
wrapped in riot and rebellion.
I would become coeval with their dreams, become
like them creators of a catechism,
and you would bend to unbraid your hair
like a heap of coins at my feet,
and whisper: "Tell me, Master,

is not this the day
we two will go, at last at
liberty, to seek the way?"

The One, the Only Book (from *As I Am Easy*)

I have seen the black Vedas,
The Koran and the Gospels,
And the books of the Mongols
On their silken boards—
All made of dust, of earth's ashes,
Of the sweet-smelling dung
That Kalmyk women use for morning fuel—
I have seen them go to the fire,
Lie down in a heap and vanish
White as widows in clouds of smoke
In order to hasten the coming
Of the One, the Only Book,
Whose pages are enormous oceans
Flickering like the wings of a blue butterfly,
And the silk thread marking the place
Where the reader rests his gaze
Is all the great rivers in a dark blue flood:
    Volga, where they sing the Stenka Razin songs at
      nighttime,
    Yellow Nile, where they worship the sun,
    Yangtse-Kiang, oozing with people,
    And mighty Mississippi, where the Yankees strut
In star-spangled trousers, yes, in pants
All covered with stars,
    And Ganges, whose dark people are trees of the mind,
    And Danube, white people in white shirts
Whose whiteness is reflected in the water,
    And Zambezi, whose people are blacker than boots,
    And stormy Ob, where they hack out their idol
And turn him face to the wall
Whenever they eat forbidden fat,
    And Thames which is boring, boring.

Race of Humanity, Reader of the Book
Whose cover bears the creator's signature,
The sky-blue letters of my name!
Yes you, careless reader,
Look up! Pay attention!
You let your attention wander
Lazily, as if you were still in catechism class.
Soon, very soon you will read
These mountain chains and these enormous oceans!
They are the One, the Only Book!
The whale leaps from its pages,
And the eagle's pinion bends the edge of a page
As it swoops across sea-waves, the breasts
Of ocean, to rest in the osprey's bed.

Night in Persia

The seashore.
Sky. Stars. I lie back tranquil.
No feathers for a pillow, and no stone:
Just a sailor's cast-off shoe.
The same shoes Samorodov wore in those Red days
When he raised revolt on the sea
And moved the ships of the Whites to Krasnovodsk—
Into Redwater.
Getting dark. It's dark.
"Comrade, lend a hand!"
An Iranian calling, cast-iron color,
Gathering brush from the ground.
I pulled his strap
And helped him hoist his load.
"Saool!" (or "thanks," as we would say).
He disappeared in the darkness.
I whispered in the darkness
The name Mekhdi.
Mekhdi?
A beetle flew out of the black
And pounding sea,

Flew straight at me,
Turned twice above my head,
Furled his wings, and settled in my hair.
He was calm and quiet first but
Suddenly began to make his sound.
He said distinctly what he had to say
In a language we both understood.
Pleased and persistent, he had his say
And we understood each other!
A pact in night and darkness
Signed by beetle sound.
Then he hoisted his wings, his sails,
And flew away.
The sea erased his sound
And the trace of a kiss on the sand.
All this happened!
Just as I've told it here.

The Dregs of Opium

Work in blind wall eyeglasses
Squats over tomorrow's lessons.
Eager to make the truths of work self-evident,
Secret corners of the sun-struck streets
Are full of shady stories, squalid lairs
Where a solitary shot rings out! No, only groans
That soon draw from the dreamer all intelligence
Of doing day-to-day what day must do.
He sucks dry-mouthed, but sucks sweet honey
And with this venom as his pilgrim staff
Sets off to find the drowsy shore of dreams.
Immediately the holy blaze of fire,
The hammer beating on the bending iron,
Everything vanishes. The armor plate of fantasy
Seals up a sober mind.
Upon these plains grow only chains,
But he hears nothing now, not the voice of the street,
Not evening, enchanting, flowers of words wasted

Yesterday, nor voices prophesying vanities,
The slow sea-sound of daily cares.
Forgotten, all of it. Work vanishes
In thought-smoke, in familiar favorite dreams . . .
But this captive in iron chains of smoke
Is caught in the cloud of his desires,
And down his sleepy road he goes
To paradise, the smokey rites of paradise,
Where people vanish. Adam is alone.
It's almost day. Dawn blisters in a crack of night
And see? A slave again. He goes to work.
But that same shore still beckons,
And in debts of iron chains he seems
A boat adrift, upon some night-smoke Volga.

Iranian Song

Down along the river, by the old Iran,
By the cool green ripple
By the deep dark bank
Where the sweet sweet waters flow,
A pair of drifters one day walking,
Walking, waving pistols, talking,
Shooting fishes as they go.
Hold it, honey . . . got 'im! Right between the eyes.
Two men walking, two men talking.
I'm almost sure I remember this right,
They made fish soup, but they didn't make it often.
"Gotta believe, it's a tin-can life!"

Way up high a plane is flying,
Magic carpet in the sky.
Where's the carpet's second cousin,
The magic tablecloth that covers itself with food?
That tablecloth has been delayed in transit,
Or maybe even landed in jail. Now I always knew
Fairy tales could come true:
Today's hard fact was once a fairy tale.

And of course I believe there's a great day coming,
But by the time it gets here I'll be six feet under!
When the great day comes and they gather over yonder
And the flags start waving up ahead,
When they yell hallelujah
I may wake up from the dead,
But by then I'll be a dusty bunch of bones.
Should I throw all my rights
In the furnace of the future?
Hey you hayfield, blast and blacken!
River, turn to stone forever!

The Civil War of 1918–1920 meant massive disruption of the Russian economy, and in the summers of 1920 and 1921 there was disastrous drought. Like many Russians during this time, Khlebnikov wandered from place to place and suffered hunger, deprivation, and disease. The poems that follow are from his notebooks dated 1920–21. They differ in style from his earlier work—these are simpler, freer, perhaps not yet fully worked. They provide one of our most moving documents of that tragic period of Russian history.

They used to have a cow
but they killed her.
Traded her for sacks of flour
and now the bread's all gone. One of the neighbors
killed her, none of the family could.
Blackie. She had heavy sides
and her udder held a full pail of milk.
She had big horns, and she really made a bellow
when she mooed for her baby in the evening.
The little girls cried.
But they all ate the little calf anyway
once they were out of horsemeat
in that village.

A boy down by the creek
caught three frogs yesterday.
They were big and fat and green

and "better than chicken"
he said to his sisters, who smiled
with glee. Last night
by the fire they chattered
cooked their frogs
and ate them.
I wonder if maybe today
they get butterfly borscht?

Roast mouse.
Their son fixed it, went and
caught them in the field.
They lie stretched out on the table,
their long dark tails.
Today it's a decent dinner,
a real good meal!
Just a while back the housewife would shudder
and holler, smash the pitcher to smithereens
if she found a mouse drowned in the cream.
But now, how silent and peaceful.
Dead mice for dinner
stretched out on the table,
dangling dark tails.

In the hut next door with the board roof
a grim-faced father
broke up the bread into breadcrumbs
with hardened fingers.
Only to look at.
It wouldn't fill a sparrow, the one
that chirped just now.
Something for eyes to eat, at least.
"Times aren't right," father muttered.
The black bread looked like topsoil

with bits of ground-up pine cone.
Provided that eyes can eat.
Mother stood by the stove.
The thin slice of a white mouth.

In the corner, mother's enormous eyes
grew dark and stared.
And what's for seconds?
For seconds? A hole in the ground
where all embrace. They will lie down
huddled together,
fathers and families:
fathers and mothers and sisters and brothers.

Dinner is served, and here's the first course
in the old iron kettle: boiled-up chaff.
It's good for scouring stomachs.
Children, come eat your boiling water
and your little bits of straw. Your soup.
The children sit down. Now you stop that
you're big kids, you stop that crying, hear?
And they all got serious faces
and nobody laughed. Nobody fooled around.
Mother stood by the stove like she used to,
but she held her face in her hand and cried.
The kids got quiet and scared
like something mysterious happened
or somebody died.
Their eyes were dark and their mouths drooped
and dinner was over.
Then the kids went away and disappeared.

It has the unassuming face of a burnt-out candle.
Fire-eye, lacking its lashes
of downpour and rain.
It burned our fields, our land,
whole populations of stalks of grain
shaken like straw.
The fields grew smokey and the grain turned
yellow as death and fell.
The grain shriveled and mice ate it.
Is the sky sick? Does the sky hurt?
Where are its watery lashes?
What became of wet weather, and pounding rain?
Furious fire-eye, burning our hayfields,
our grasses and gardens,
constantly burning, its cloud brows gone.
People sat down in a daze
to wait for a miracle, and
there wasn't one. They were waiting to die.
This was sky-blue disaster.
This was drought. After a run of caring years,
this changeling.
Now everything is different—grain and rain—
and denies the farmer's labor.
Didn't the plowman's sweating hand
scatter good seed that spring?
Didn't the farmer stand all spring
looking up, hoping for rain?
Fire-eye. Naked
golden glare,
burning the fields
of the Volga plain.
The fires of heaven were merciless.
They burned four regions beginning with S.

"Eat it up, puppy,
and hope you won't die!"
a mother shouted to her youngest

then ran from the farmhouse.
The sound of laughing and crying
came from the hayloft.
Her eyes flutter like black moths
caught in her brows.
What's that noise from the ravine
in the woods, those feet
moving forward?
Downpours of eyelashes
vanished that summer . . .

Dust in the air near the ravine
in the woods.
A crowd rushed out to the green hills,
to the three tall pines,
all of them hurrying, anxious—
sticks in their hands,
long beards at angles,
anxious and hurrying,
running and rushing, all of them,
grown-ups and children, it was hunger that did it.
They were trying to find the holy dirt,
the dirt you can eat just like bread
and never get sick from.
People were running. Rushing.
You're all we have left, now that
everything's different!
Earth! Dirt!

Hunger herded humanity.
Men, women, children,
they fill the ravine
rushing to find the holy dirt
that makes do for bread.
Dirt, our silent savior

beneath the roots of century pines.
And at that very moment scientists' minds
were striving toward other worlds,
seeking to fashion a dream of life
out of earths made fertile by thought.

Bow! Wow! Wow!
Black bunch
Bow! Wow! Wow!
Running dogs
Bow! Wow! Wow!
Rage in snow
Bow! Wow! Wow!
Outside town
Bow! Wow! Wow!
Rip the dead
Bow! Wow! Wow!
Drag someone's leg
Bow! Wow! Wow!
Drag someone's arm
Bow! Wow! Wow!
In snout in belly
In blood in snow.

Today Mount Mashuk is a hound dog,
All white, with clumps of birchtree sparks.
A bird against it, freezing cold,
Flies south toward Piatagorsk.

. . . Flies over a spark-spewing train,
Forgets the stillness of mountains
Where autumn stoops to glean
What grain still lies in the hollows.

And then what? A mindless return,
Though the poor thing's wings are frozen.
Their eyes are prickly as hay-rakes,
Their eyes are wintry and cold.

Commerce has speeded their lives up,
Turned their eyes grim as gunshot.
And now they sport a pair of ears
To hear the hucksters hawk their wares.

[September 7, 1921]

The year the girls first called me "gramps"—
giving me the go-by in their voices and acting
as if I was old—they treated me badly
because of my body, a plate not bashfully
dished, maybe, but still not eaten up yet,
in the arms of long nights
in that healing-house the Narzan spring
I sluiced down my body,
got stronger and stronger
and pulled myself into a man
once more. Veins reappeared in my hands,
my chest grew stronger,
and soft silky hairs
started to cover my chin.

The lice had blind faith, and they prayed to me.
Every morning they would congregate on my clothes,
every morning I visited punishment upon them
and listened to them crackle and die.
But they kept on returning again and again
in a quiet worshipful wave.

The years 1920–1922 were a time of enormous hardship in Russia, but also years of an enormous surge of creativity in all the arts. "I remember shaking with excitement all the time," Sergei Eisenstein wrote, thinking of his work in the theater during those years. For Khlebnikov too this was the period of his greatest achievement. In the midst of privation and the upheaval of civil war and famine, he had his most prophetic visions of the future. They found shape in essays like "The Radio of the Future" and "Ourselves and Our Buildings," in the grandiose conceptions of Zangezi *and* The Tables of Destiny, *and in a series of remarkable, mature poems: powerful, direct, inspired by vision and a sense of the accomplishment of his own destiny.*

Once more, Khlebnikov invokes Walt Whitman as a companion and brother, a poet who shared his convinced sense of the wholeness and interconnectedness of all things, the Whitman who wrote:

> *To me the converging objects of the universe*
> *perpetually flow,*
> *All are written to me, and I must get what the*
> *writing means.*

The poems that follow are a few examples of Khlebnikov's attempts to get what the writing means.

Russia, I give you my divine
white brain. Be me. Be Khlebnikov.
I have sunk a foundation deep in the minds
of your people, I have laid down an axis.
I have built a house on a firm foundation.
"We are Futurians."

And I did all that as a beggarman,
a thief, a man with a curse on his head.

Attentively I read the springtime thoughts of the Divinity in
designs on the speckled feet of tree-toads,
Homer shaken by the awful wagon of a great war, the way
a glass shakes at the passing of a wagon.
I have the same Neanderthal skull, the same curving
forehead as you, old Walt.

The Solitary Player

While Akhmatova wept and her poems poured out
Over Tsarskoe Selo,
I have to unwind the enchantress' thread
And drag myself like a drowsy corpse through the desert:
All about me, impossibility lay dying.
I was a worn-out actor, a poor player
Shuffling heedlessly on.
But meanwhile in dark caves
The curly head of that subterranean bull
Kept up its bloody chomping, devouring men
In the smoke of insolent threats.
And wrapped in the moon's inclination
Like the tardy traveler in his drowsy cloak,
In dreams I leapt upon the precipice
And moved from cliff to cliff.
I moved like a blind man, until
Freedom's wind directed me,
Beat me with slanting rain.
And I cut the bull's head from the hulking meat and the
bones,
And set it upon the wall
Like a fighter for the truth, and shook it in the world's face:
Here it is, look!
Here is that curly head the crowd once blazed for!

And with horror
I understood—no one could see me.
I would have to sow eyes.
My task was to be a sower of eyes!

Let the plowman leave his furrow
To watch the crow that flies across his field
And let him say: that cry contains
The fall of Troy,
Achilles' howling anger
And the weeping queen.
As it circles (its jaws
Are black) above his head,
Let a dusty table, where there is lots of dust,
Pattern the dust into circles, curves
Like the gray insides of a wave,
And let some schoolboy say: that dust
Is Moscow, there, and that's
Peking, or a cowfield near Chicago.
Capital cities have circled the earth
In the mesh of a fisherman's net.
The sound of various worlds produces
A planet chicagoed in knots of dust.
And let a bride, who would not want to see
Mourning bands beneath her fingernails,
Scrape the dust from under them and murmur:
Here in this dust burn living suns
And worlds no mind dares comprehend.
Her nails wear shrouds of dying flesh.
I believe that even the light of Sirius must fail
To pierce the dark beneath a fingernail.

Suppose I make a timepiece of humanity,
Demonstrate the movement of the century hand—
Will war not wither like an unused letter, drop

From your alphabet, vanish from our little gap
Of time? Humanity has piles, got by rocking
In armchairs forever and ever, compressing
The mainspring of war. I tell you, the future is
Coming, and upon it my superhuman dreams.
I know you are true believing wolves—
I squeeze my shots into the bull's-eye like yours—
But can't you hear fate's needle, rustling
In her wonderworking seams?
The force of my thoughts will inundate
The structures of existing states—
I'll reveal to the serfs of old stupidity
The magic city of Kitezh, risen from its lake.
When the band of Presidents of Planet Earth
Will feed our appalling hunger with a new crust,
Then the rough lug nuts of existing states
Will yield easily to the turn of our wrench.
And when the bearded lady
Throws the long-awaited stone,
That, you will say,
Is what we've been wanting
For centuries. Ticking timepiece of humanity!
Move like the arrow of my thoughts!
Grow as governments destroy themselves, grow
Through this book, let Planet Earth
Be sovereignless at last! PRESPLANEARTH alone
Will be our sovereign song.
I tell you, the universe is the scratch
Of a match on the face of the calculus,
And my thoughts are a picklock at work
On a door, and behind it someone is dying . . .

[January 28, 1922]

OK, Graylegs,
You're pulling Planet Earth, so
How 'bout a little giddup and go?

A plow of stars
Hitched to your traces,
A whip of dreams—
And we're off to the races!

I write poems about it all
To put oats in your pail.

What would you say to ancestral hay?
It's a special honor, so don't say neigh.

I'm not making fun
Of your coat of gray;
I love you, old girl,
And I just wanna play!

I'll fill your old pail
With a full cup of oats
Before the universal brawl
To conquer the skies.

Like cool water flowing
I say where I'm going
And describe the great numbers
That feed on my thoughts.

I fed you so we could
Catch hold of our sail,
Though of course you like oats
And a full water pail.

I fed you because:

My soul is a seer
Who has seen in the skies
The constellations beginning to rise
And the thunderstorm fly like a bird,

White-maned—our friend, you know?—
Whose mane shines bright in the mountain snow.
"OURS," say letters of clouds in the sky,
And that means . . . keep your powder dry.

OK, Graylegs. You're pulling
Planet Earth. So take care.
Koltsov's Graylegs.
Tolstoy's Old Gray Mare.

The Milky Way!
Who's calling me up there?

[February 2, 1922]

A herd of horses shod with Hours
Jangling like thunder, wheel in a field.
Their rugged bodies are rank with Time,
Their flashing eyes ablaze with Days.

Fictions

Khlebnikov, 1912

Khlebnikov writes in 1919: "In Mrs. Laneen *I wanted to discover the 'infinitesimals' of artistic language." All the fictions in this section, plays and prose, are in a sense attempts to make that discovery: What are the building blocks of artistic creation, Khlebnikov asks, and how can they be fitted together? How, in particular, does the accumulation of details go to create the perception of an event? The pieces in this section are varied in style and genre, but they illustrate this central preoccupation. The two small plays,* Mrs. Laneen *and* The World in Reverse, *seem like sketches for more elaborate treatment, but both are strictly schematic and derive from theater experiments of the time: they are attempts at interior monologue, following the experiments of Maeterlinck in* The Intruder, Interior, *and* The Blind, *and especially of Evreinov, whose monodrama,* The Performance of Love, *similar in style to* Mrs. Laneen, *was published in 1910 in the same journal as Khlebnikov's poems "Incantation by Laughter" and "The Tangled Wood."*

The fantasy "K" is, in its own way, a compendium of the devices of science fiction written well before the development of that genre but, for all its hallucinatory details, is a first-person narration describing the perceptions of the narrator, as are Mrs. Laneen *and "October on the Neva." The fact that one is fantasy, one a play, and the other a historical memoir is less important than the basic matter of what and how we perceive and record. Khlebnikov addresses the question of what constitutes an event—in history as well as in personal, emotional life—and at what level of perception we might possibly distinguish the objective from the subjective.*

"Nikolai" is also a first-person narration, but here, as in "Usa-Gali," Khlebnikov writes more conventionally, as he focusses on the

vital question, for him, of man's relationship to his natural environment. The presentation of two such "natural" men, in a traditionally objective narrative frame that distances us from them and their behavior and thus offers them as models, points to Khlebnikov's intense concern for a world in danger of destruction.

Mrs. Laneen

CHARACTERS: Voice of Sight
Voice of Hearing
Voice of Reason
Voice of Thought
Voice of Recollection
Voice of Conjecture
Voice of Will
Voice of Joy
Voice of Intellect
Voice of Consciousness
Voice of Touch
Voice of Terror
Voice of Attention

(The action takes place during two days in Mrs. Laneen's life, a week apart.)

(Twilight. The scene takes place in front of a blank wall.)

ACT ONE

Voice of Sight It's stopped raining. There are a few raindrops still hanging on the bending ends of the darkening garden.

Voice of Hearing Silence. You can hear someone opening the gate. Someone is walking along the garden path.

Voice of Reason Which way are they going?

Voice of Thought There's only one way you can go here.

Voice of Sight Someone has frightened the birds. They've all scattered.

Voice of Thought It's the same person who opened the gate.

Voice of Hearing The air is full of frightened birdcalls. And loud footsteps.

Voice of Sight Yes, someone is coming closer. But he walks very slowly.

Voice of Recollection It's Doctor Loos. He's been here before, it wasn't too long ago.

Voice of Sight He's dressed in black from head to foot. And his hat is pulled way down, you can barely see his laughing blue eyes. His reddish moustache is turned up at the ends today, just like it is every day. His face is flushed and full of self-confidence. He's smiling, his lips look as if they are saying something.

Voice of Hearing He's saying: "Hello, Mrs. Laneen." He's also saying: "Nice weather we're having today, isn't it?"

Voice of Sight His lips smile with assurance. He seems to be expecting an answer. His face is beginning to look serious. Now his face and his mouth seem to be relaxing and smiling.

Voice of Reason He's pretending to apologize for the silence. But I won't say anything.

Voice of Sight His mouth is forming an ingratiating expression.

Voice of Hearing He's asking it again. He's asking: "How do you feel?"

Voice of Reason Say something to him. Say: "I feel fine."

Voice of Sight His eyebrows are quivering with pleasure. His forehead is wrinkled.

Voice of Hearing He's saying: "I hope . . ."

Voice of Reason Don't listen to what he says. He'll be saying goodbye in just a minute. He'll be leaving soon.

Voice of Hearing But he still keeps on saying something.

Voice of Sight His lips never stop moving. Doesn't he look kind! And polite! And he seems so interested!

Voice of Conjecture He's talking about something important.

Voice of Reason Let him talk. He's not getting any answer from me.

Voice of Will He's not getting any answer from me.

Voice of Sight He's surprised. He's making a gesture with his hand. An uncertain gesture.

Voice of Reason You've got to shake his hand. What an intolerable ritual!

Voice of Sight His black hat floats in the air, it goes straight up, and then it goes down again onto his light brown hair. He turned around, he moved his straight black shoulders, there's a speck of dandruff on one of them. And now he's going away.

Voice of Joy At last.

Voice of Sight You can barely see him—that dark figure, a gleam beyond the trees.

Voice of Hearing I can hear his footsteps at the end of the garden.

Voice of Reason He won't come here again.

Voice of Hearing The gate slammed shut.

Voice of Reason This bench is cold and damp after the rain, and everything's quiet. That man has gone away, and now life is returning.

Voice of Sight The garden is wet. Somebody has made a circular mark. Footprints. The leaves are wet, the ground is wet.

Voice of Intellect People here are very unhappy. There is evil here, but no one does anything about it.

Voice of Consciousness Thought conquers all. Loneliness is thought's companion. You have to keep your distance from people.

Voice of Sight Pigeons fly into the garden. Pigeons fly away.

Voice of Hearing The gate is opening again.

Voice of Will I won't say a word. I am keeping my distance from people.

ACT TWO

Voice of Touch My hands are shaking. My fingers are touching the cold knots on this jacket. My arms are prisoners, and my feet are bare and I can feel the cold from the stone floor.

Voice of Hearing Silence. I am here.

Voice of Sight Blue and red circles. Spinning around, and moving from place to place. It's dark. A light.

Voice of Hearing More steps. One, then another. They're loud, because it's so quiet everywhere.

Voice of Terror Who is it?

Voice of Attention They went away. They changed direction. Now they're coming back.

Voice of Reason This way. That means me. They're coming for me.

Voice of Hearing They've stopped. Everything's quiet.

Voice of Terror The door will open soon.

Voice of Hearing The key is scraping in the lock.

Voice of Terror The key is turning.

Voice of Reason It's them.

Voice of Consciousness I'm afraid.

Voice of Will But I still won't say a word. Not a word.

Voice of Sight The door is open.

Voice of Hearing Here's what they're saying: "You're a sick woman. Please come with us. It's doctor's orders."

Voice of Will No.

Voice of Consciousness I won't say a word.

Voice of Sight They're all around me.

Voice of Touch There's a hand on my shoulder.

Voice of Recollection . . . white, it used to be white.

Voice of Touch My hair just brushed the floor.

Voice of Recollection . . . black. Long and black.

Voice of Hearing They're saying: "Hold her head! Take her by the shoulders! Got her? Let's go!"

Voice of Consciousness They are carrying her away. It's all over. World-wide evil.

Voice of Hearing I can hear someone saying: "Haven't they gotten that patient moved yet?" "Not yet."

Voice of Consciousness Everything's dead. Everything's dying.

[pub. 1913]

The World in Reverse

SCENE ONE

Olly Imagine, just imagine. Here I am a man of seventy already, and what do they do? They lay me down, they tie me up, they babify me, they sprinkle me with smelly stuff. What am I, a doll?

Polly Don't get upset now. Of course you're not a doll.

Olly Horses in black sheets with drippy eyes and droopy ears. And that carriage! It goes so slow and it's all white and me in it just like a vegetable. Lie down and shut up and keep your legs straight, keep your eyes open and keep 'em on the neighbors and count the number of times the family yawns, and those fake forget-me-nots messing up my pillow and passersby poking around. Well I tell you I got out of *that* one fast! To hell with them all! I climbed right into a cab and got here as fast as I could, not a hat or a coat, and all of them shouting: Grab him! Grab him! Grab him!

Polly So you got out of it? Well, if that isn't something! What a bright boy you are! A soaring miracle, and that's the truth.

Olly Oh but you have to let me rest. You can hide me right here in the closet. All these clothes, well they can come out, what are they all still here for anyway? Now this one, this one I wore the day I got promoted, who was it now? God rest his soul. Old Georgie, that's it, it was him was in charge and me they made councillor. This was the one. I got all done up and went to the head office, here's the crease on the cloth where my medal went, good cloth, you don't find this kind of goods about nowadays, and this little place here where the sword hooked on, oh he was a great one, I tell you, a great one that tailor, down on Ocean Avenue. Ah god, will you look at that, it's a moth, grab it now, quick! *(They chase the moth, hopping about and clapping their hands after it.)* The nasty thing! *(They both catch it at once.)* I remember he kept on saying I'll sew you up a purse out of this, he'd say, a purse of the best goods going, it'll never wear out, he'd say. Tight as a purse, he'd say, and you fill my purse when you pay me, he'd say, and fill it full, I don't care if you wear out *that,* he'd say. And now there's a moth at it! And this is your wedding dress, darling, remember? Church of the Holy Cross. Now we'll sprinkle everything all over with strong tobacco, that's what they used to use, and this other stuff, the smelly stuff, the smell makes you want to start crying, now we'll lay it all out in the trunk and lock it up good, and get us a good big lock, you know what I mean, a big one, and the pillows, you know, right on top, make sure its the feather ones—I'm tired, darling, I'm terribly tired, gimme a minute, so's I can take a little rest, there's something pounding right here at my heart, it's all those cats, you know, they come clawing and scratching away at your heart—and first thing you know all those awful things are right out in the open—the carriage, and the flowers, and the relatives all singing hymns, and oh, you know, it's not easy, darling, not easy at all. *(He sniffs.)* So if they show up tell them he's way the hell and gone and he can't come back anyway because of the doctor, he said he was dead already, and here's the paper, you know, you just take this paper, shove it right into their faces and tell them they already took me, the damn fools, he's gone to the cemetery already and it's no business of yours, you say, and I'm glad he's gone, you can say, but the paper's the main thing, you know, they give up when they see a piece of paper, and now I . . . *(he smiles)* I gotta take a little rest.

Polly Darling, your eyes are all wet from weeping, you've had such a terrible time of it, let me wipe your poor eyes with my little hanky. *(She stands on tiptoes and wipes away his tears.)* Rest easy, my old darling, rest easy. There's none of them worth all the upset, so smile, now, give me a smile! Here, I'll pour you a nice little berry brandy, you drink that up, that'll fix you, and here's your peppermint pills, and that candle now, take the one in the black candlestick, it'll last you better. *(There's a knock at the door.)*

Olly And sprinkle this stuff in the trunk. Keeps off the moths. *(He jumps in with the candlestick in his hand. She locks him in with a victorious flourish, gives a look about, and marches into the hallway with her hands on her hips.)*

Voice in the Hallway Good morning! M-m-m ah-ah-ah bz-bz-bz Pa . . . Nik . . . Nik . . . Hey ah ah?

Polly Well, God rest his soul! You see, ahmic, mic, mic . . . *(She starts to cry.)* They came and got him. Covered him right up, and he was still alive, the lovely old darling!

Voice in the Hallway You mean? ah, ah, ah . . . The old lady's touched, she's off her rocker. Ah-ah? That's awful peculiar, you could almost say this is something, now, couldn't you?

Polly He's dead, so help me, believe me, he's dead. Only half an hour ago, now why should I lie to you, an old lady like me with a foot in her own grave already. No, he's dead, he's dead, I swear to god, now what about you, are you all in a hurry? Got someplace to get to, I'll bet you. Am I right? And if not, you just come right in, come in, sit down, rest up if you're tired, of course you are, and I'll just go light a candle, you know that's the custom, and you, you just rest, take a seat in the parlor, smoke if you wish, but the one thing I'll never give up is this key. Not if you put me to a thousand deaths! You can cut me to pieces, you can tear me apart, you can tie my fair white body to a herd of wild horses, you'll never get this key and that's all we're going to say about *that*. Now don't be nervous, just take a seat in the parlor . . .

Voice in the Hallway She's bats . . .

Polly Now what's your hurry, don't you go running off on me like that! Well I never. He's gone. And this sure is something. *(She bangs on the closet with the key.)* He's gone. Goddam spy, he's gone, what I did is I did this and then that . . .

Olly What? He's gone?

Polly All gone, darling.

Olly Well thank God for that. You have to give him credit for that, for going, I mean. Here I am sitting in here and thinking how is this all going to turn out, and wouldn't you know it all turned out for the best.

Polly And of course I says to him, "You must be in a hurry, I says, you look like you got someplace to get to." And it never occurred to him what's going on, God love him! You can come out now, darling. Oh there's the door again! Well I'm not even going to open it this time, I'm just going to tell them I'm sick. Sick, I'll say, sick enough to die! Who is it? *(A muffled reply.)* I'm sick, you can't come in, I'm sick!

Unknown Voice But I'm the doctor!

Polly Oh, I'm so sick, I have this strange disease, every time I see a doctor I grab hold of a broomstick or a poker, or a pail of water, or maybe even something worse!

Voices Outside the Door What? I suppose so . . . How could it happen? God help her! So what should we do? She can go take a ride on her broomstick . . .

Polly They're gone, darling, my brave darling, they're all gone.

Olly I can't seem to hear too well . . .

Polly I got after them with a broomstick, what else could they do, of course they're gone. *(She opens the closet door and sets the table.)* Let's go back to the country, shall we? It's awful, people singing hymns, people we don't know, horses in hats . . .

SCENE TWO

(An old house in the country. Ancient pinetrees, birches, a pond. Turkeys and chickens. The two of them are taking a walk.)

Olly Oh I'm so glad we left! What was life coming to: having to hide in your own house . . . By the way, I keep meaning to ask you, do you dye your hair?

Polly Why do you ask? Do you?

Olly Not at all, but I remembered it as gray, and now its gotten quite dark.

Polly You know you're absolutely right. And your moustache is quite dark too, you look as if you'd lost forty years, and look at your cheeks, why they're just like they say in the fairy tales, snow-white and rose-red. And your eyes! I swear, they're all sparkle and fire! You're a dashing young man, just like they say in the song! What do you suppose it all means?

Olly Oh look, we're in luck, there's our next-door neighbor, he's come over to visit and he gets our little Nadia into conversations about natural selection, no less. You'd better keep an eye on them, that could turn out very badly.

Polly Yes, yes, I know, I am quite aware of what's going on, believe you me. And our young Petey is always hanging around now and does nothing. It's high time to send him off to school, don't you think? Maybe he'll learn something.

Olly He can still learn what he has to from his young friends, boys will be boys and he'll get kicked and beaten up and that will take the bloom of youth off him. God forbid he should turn out to be a mama's boy.

Polly Well I certainly don't think that's very likely! You remember, running away without a hat and the coachman and the friends and relations and then he grew up and the horsehair crest waving on top of that bronze helmet and the way those sullen eyes looked in that hard soldier's face, they burned like fire it was so sad and so sweet and now a little dark fuzz on his upper lip, you can barely make it out, like sandpaper, oh it's the worse time of all: you take your eyes off them for barely a moment and it's all over. *(Little Petey runs up with a rifle, carrying a blackbird.)*

Petey I killed a crow!

Polly But why, why, why? What did you have to do it for?

Petey He was croaking at me.

Polly Well young man, you'll just have your supper tonight in your room, all by yourself. And from now on you remember: whenever you kill a bird, you kill something in yourself.

Petey I'm not hungry, I already had some milk at Molly's.

Polly At Molly's? You're leaving here tomorrow!

Olly Yes, young man, tomorrow! And very very early in the morning, too.

Petey And she gave me a piece of black bread.

Olly It's high time you went into the service!

Petey What kind of service? It depends on who. I don't mind servicing somebody if I really like them.

Olly That's a nice thing to hear! Well, look who's here, the origin of the species himself. Always very nice to see you I'm sure. Nina, dear, it's the young man from next door! Now correct me if I'm wrong, but aren't monkeys supposed to have a bone somewhere that's shaped like a key? Of course we're none of us scholars here, but we old folks certainly respect the mind of a man with a good education.

Polly Why—they're gone! . . . Where did they go?

Olly It looks like they've gone to the gazebo. That's a dangerous little neighbor we've got.

Polly The gazebo, hmm? Well it's high time, high time, believe me.

(Nina appears, radiant.)

Nina He's the one! He's the one! *(Answering the unspoken question.)* Yes! Yes! He did! he did! He started off talking about

Darwin and all of a sudden very innocently he was saying "The sun is in his golden carriage, may I have your hand in marriage . . ." and he seemed oh a totally changed person and he began kissing and licking my hand.

Olly Oh I'm so glad, so very glad, I want you to be very happy, healthy, wealthy, and wise. Also don't ever go too easy on him.

Nina Oh I know all about that already, way back when we used to sit together out in the garden on the bench where he carved our initials in the green paint and we used to watch the beautiful showers of shooting stars and the whip-poorwill whistled in the distance and all the clamor of the earth had grown still.

Olly Our time then, their time now, your time soon—that's the way it is in this world, everything changes.

Nina See there he is now standing under that tree. I'll go tell him yes. Yes? *(She takes Olly's hand.)*

Olly M—m—m.

SCENE THREE

(A boat on the river. Olly is dressed in an army uniform.)

Olly We are dear, dear friends, that's all, shy seekers after togetherness, we want to be close to each other and we are divers for pearls in the ocean of our eyes, we are dear, dear friends. And the boat drifts along, casting its shadow on the current; we bend over the edge and we see our own faces reflected, there among the dancing clouds in the water, all caught in the river's drifting net when they fall from the skies: and noonday whispers in our ears, "Oh children, children!" it says. And we—we are the freshness of midnight.

SCENE FOUR

(Polly walks by carrying a book bag; she meets Olly. He starts upstairs, whispering a prayer.)

Polly You got your Greek now?

Olly Yes.

Polly We got Russian.

(A few hours later. They meet again.)

Polly What did you get?

Olly Zero. Like Mucius and Scaevola I sailed across the sea of low marks and like Manlius I sacrificed myself. I jumped head-first through the hole in the zero.

Polly Bye-bye.

SCENE FIVE

(Polly and Olly, silent and solemn, are wheeled by in baby carriages. They hold balloons in their hands.)

[pub. 1913]

Usa-Gali

Usa-Gali was a falconer, a hunter, and every now and then a thief. If they caught him he would act like it was all in fun. "You mean I can't?" he would say. "I thought I could!" If he saw a lark asleep in the open steppe, Usa-Gali would crawl up to it and pin its tail to the ground, and the bird would wake up captured. An eagle was perched on a haystack. Gali moved silently toward the stack with a long rope that ended in a noose. The watchful eagle sees the hoop of hair. Full of suspicion he raises himself, ready to fly away, but he's caught already, beating his black wings, flapping and screaming. Usa-Gali jumps from behind the haystack and reels in the poor prince of the sky, a black captive with talons of iron; his wingspread reached over seven feet. Usa-Gali rides proudly through the steppe. That eagle would live for a long time in captivity, sharing his food with sheep dogs.

One time he was being chased, and a whole troop of men on horseback surrounded him. Gali wheeled his horse in the middle of the trap, but there was no way out. And so what does he do? He turned his horse and galloped directly at one of the horsemen. The horseman didn't know what to do and turned his horse flank to. Gali whirled his bullwhip, stunned the poor horse with a terrific wallop on the forehead. The horse fell to his knees and Usa-Gali galloped off. It was a wicked wallop and knocked the horse unconscious. They remembered that in the steppe for a long time, the stunned horse with his broken saddle girth and the horseman flat on his back.

In those days the Ukrainian oxcart drivers traveled in wagon trains, and they used to cover their loads with huge pieces of felt to keep them dry. Their oxen plodded along, constantly moving their wet black lips and swishing away the flies. Some of the hunters used to sneak behind the drivers, then suddenly gallop up and shove the end of the felt cover under one knee and make a dash with it off into the steppe. The drivers weren't dumb, so they started tying the felt covers to the wagons with long pieces of rope. That was when Usa-Gali tried it.

Of course once the rope was played out he was pulled off his horse, and he hit the ground so hard he broke his arm. The drivers all came running, and they took it out on him something good. "Had enough?" they kept asking him. "Enough," he said. "Enough, man, enough." But he couldn't say it very loud. That little game cost him a couple of ribs.

The bullwhip, which is a close cousin to the bolo they use further north, was something he was a real expert with; he used it the way the Kirghiz tribesmen do. He used it to hunt wolves. His trained eagles were more relentless than Borzois, and they would track the wolf out into the steppe and follow him till he was worn out and didn't care anymore what happened to him.

Then the obedient ambler would quicken his pace to a gallop, and Gali would lean down and finish off the wolf with his bullwhip. By then the poor animal was worn out from the unequal contest.

Pity the lone wolf!

One time they found him with a long switch, very proud of himself, driving a whole herd of bustards ahead of him.

"Usa-Gali, what are you doing?"

"Froze their wings," he answered offhand. "I sell them a little bit at a time."

That was once after an ice storm.

That was Usa-Gali for you.

The rest stop. A white horse grazing nearby. A flock of wood pigeons drifts down the wind. Swans shone in the bright blueness of the sky, like the edge of another world. Small white bustards were feeding on a sandy hillock.

The wood pigeons suddenly flutter up out of the grass and fly away. The murmur of conversation, someone telling a story. It's the start of the evening meal. Meanwhile some geese overhead had drawn a thin stripe right down the middle of the sky; the flock looked like a dragon kite. It disappeared somewhere far away, an endless thread; maybe that makes it easier for them to fly. The geese began to call to one another and their formation changed shape again; now they looked like the Milky Way, only dark. Meanwhile the wind had risen, and a steppe swallow's nest began to swing more heavily; it looked like a warm mitten hung up on the willow tree. A harrier hawk drifted by, all black with a beautiful silvery head.

Crows and magpies. They're a good sign, they cheer you up.

"Listen"—someone was telling a story about a Turkish woman, a captive. "She used to go out into the field and lie down, and put her ear right up against the ground, and when you asked her what she was doing she used to say: 'I'm listening to them say Mass in heaven. It sounds real good!' "

The Russians were all standing around in a circle. Usa-Gali was there too, only off to one side eating something. You hardly noticed him. He was a real creature of the steppe. Uruss builds steamships, Uruss builds roads, he doesn't even notice the life all around him in the steppe. The Russian is not to be trusted, he's an infidel.

If you listened hard to the sound of the wild geese, you could hear them saying "We salute you! Those who are fated to die salute you!"

[pub. 1913]

Nikolai

Events are strange: sometimes you can move calmly past something that has terror written all over it, and at other times it's just the opposite: you stop to look for a deep, hidden meaning in an inconsequential event. One time I was walking down the street and stopped when I saw a crowd collected around a loaded freight wagon.

"What's happening?" I asked a passerby.

"See for yourself," he said with a laugh. And what was happening was, in the dead silence, an old black horse stood beating its hoof on the roadway in a regular rhythm. All the other horses nearby were listening to him, their heads bowed, silent, motionless. In that hoofbeat you could make out an idea, a grasp of fate and a command, and all the other horses bowed their heads and paid attention. A crowd soon gathered and stayed until the driver showed up from somewhere, grabbed the reins, pulled the horse up sharply and drove on.

But that old black horse had dully deciphered destiny and his companions had bowed their heads and listened, and the incident stayed in my mind.

A wandering life is full of hard knocks, but also of magic moments that make up for it. My meeting Nikolai was one of them. I doubt you'd pay much attention to him if you met him. Only his suntanned forehead and chin would give him away. His eyes, too openly expressive of nothing, might tell you that he was a hunter, indifferent to human society and even bored by it.

He was a loner, one who had his own life, and his own death.

He kept clear of people. He was like a house in the country shut off from the main highway by a high wall, one that faced the back road.

He was a plain and simple man, taciturn, guarded, and unsociable.

He could seem frankly ill-tempered. When he had been drinking he became crude and offensive to people he knew, constantly pestering them for money, but—and this was strange—he experienced a wave of tenderness for children: I wonder if this wasn't because they had not yet grown into people? I have known this trait in others, too. He would gather a crowd of kids around him and spend whatever spare change he had on cheap candies for them, cakes or cookies, the kind of things that line the cashier's counter in small shops. Perhaps he was trying to say: Look, all you people, why not treat each other the way I treat these children, and since such tenderness was so far removed from his trade, his silent sermon had more of an effect on me than the sermons of some other teacher with a worldwide reputation. At such times his direct eyes seemed to shine with some simple, uncompromising notion.

But who can really read the soul of an unsociable gray-haired hunter, the uncompromising adversary of boar and wild geese? He always made me think of the uncompromising verdict on life rendered by a dying Tatar, who left a note with the short but intriguing phrase: "To hell with the whole world."

For the Tatars, the man who wrote that was an apostate from the faith, a traitor; the Russian authorities, of course, looked on him as a dangerous hothead. I must confess I myself have more than once felt like adding my name to a note like that, full of indifference and despair. But that silent display of freedom from the iron laws of life and its harsh uncompromising truth, and that old hickory tree with the flowers of the field gathered at his feet—both are deep images. Both men possessed a simple and uncompromising notion and preserved it, come what may, in their honest eyes.

In one particular photo album, a very old one, among old men stooped and past their prime with medals on their chests, among affected old ladies wearing gold chains on their wrists, all posed beside the same open book, you may one day come across the faded image of a modest man with an unremarkable face, his hair combed with a plain straight part, wearing a straight beard and holding a double-barreled rifle on his knees.

If you ask who the man in the faded photograph is, they will say that's Nikolai. It will be a short answer and I suspect there will be no details forthcoming. A slight shadow on your interlocuter's face will indicate that this man is someone special, someone not entirely unknown.

I knew the man. One possible way to relate to people, in my opinion, is to think of them as different illuminations of one and the same head carved in white marble. That way, the endless variety of human faces becomes merely the contemplation of the same eyes and forehead in various illuminations, the play of light and shadow over the same stone head, always the same for old and young, for doers and dreamers, in an endless number of repetitions.

And Nikolai too, of course, was simply one of the many possible illuminations of that same hair and eyes of white stone. But is it ever possible for someone *not* to be?

His hunting exploits have been described by many. When he was asked to bring in a certain animal, he would simply ask "how many?"—taciturnity was his striking feature—and vanish. And then, God knows how, he would appear with exactly the number that had been requested. The wild hogs of the region knew him as a quiet and terrible enemy.

Chyorni—a region of shallows full of reeds—was a place he knew like the back of his hand. If it were possible to see into the souls of the feathered inhabitants at the mouth of the Volga, who knows what terrible image of this hunter would be stamped there! Whenever their cries rang out over a deserted shore, did that mournful sound not carry the news that the barque of Bird-Death was moored once more among them? Did he not appear to them as a terrifying creature with supernatural powers, with his double-barreled shotgun and his gray peaked cap?

This dreadful, implacable divinity appeared even on remote shores: black flock or white, long cries heralded the death of their companions. And yet pity had a place in his heart: he never touched a nest and would leave fledglings alone: they heard only his departing step.

He was taciturn and secretive, but more often uncommunicative, and only those to whom he had shown a corner of his soul realized that he had already condemned life and had the "noble savage's" contempt for human destiny as a whole. Perhaps the state of his soul can best be understood if we say that this is how the soul of "nature" would condemn innovation if the life of this hunter was to be its passage from the world of the "dying" into the world which is coming to take its place; with a parting glance at blizzards of ducks, at the wilderness, a world whose seas were stained with the blood of red geese, to move into a land of white stone foundation-pilings pounded into the riverbed, the fragile lace of iron bridges, anthill cities, a powerful but cold and gloomy world.

He was simple, direct, uncompromising in a somewhat coarse way. He was a patient nurse: he knew how to sit quietly by a bedside and always took care of his sick friends; and where gentleness toward the weak was concerned, or readiness to protect them, any medieval knight in armor and a plumed helmet might have reason to envy him.

He set out to hunt in the following manner: He got into his boat with two dogs he had raised himself and set off downstream with his sail cleated. Sometimes he rowed, sometimes he had to tow. I must tell you that the Volga has a treacherous wind that will blow offshore in the middle of a dead calm and overturn the careless fisherman who hasn't managed to cast loose his sail. Once they had reached their destination the boat was turned upside down and during the day it served as a shelter, supported on iron rods. Then began the long hunter's day near a campfire, until it was time to leave for an evening meal. The quiet, intelligent dogs were fed in the boat, which was always redolent of all the game to be found along the Volga: black cormorants and the drying haunch of a wild hog lay in a heap with bustards of all descriptions.

The wolves would begin their quiet howl: "That's them getting ready to leave," "that's them leaving."

His desire was to die far away from people, with whom he was completely disillusioned. He spent time among people, but he despised them. His was a cruel trade. He felt at home with the nonpeople he hunted, and among them he must surely have been some sort of cruel prince who brings death; but in the struggle between people and the nonpeople he was on the side of the latter. In a similar way Melnikov, while persecuting the

Old Believers, nevertheless wrote *In the Mountains* and *In the Forests*. There is in fact no way to imagine him except as Perun of the Birds, cruel, yet keeping faith with his followers and conscious that they possessed a certain beauty.

He had people he was able to call friends; but the more his soul came out of its "shell," the more strongly and thoroughly did he destroy the equality of the friendship to his own advantage; he would become arrogant, and the friendship began to resemble a temporary truce between two warring parties. The least incident could trigger the break, and then he would fix upon you a look that said "No, you're not one of us," and become cold and distant.

Not many people were aware that he did not, strictly speaking, belong to the race of men. His thoughtful eyes, his tight-lipped mouth—for some twenty to thirty years, after all, he had been high priest in the temple of Slaughter and Death. Between the city and the wilderness there is the same axis, the same difference, as between devil and demon. Reason begins at the point where we are able to choose in favor of good or evil. Our hunter had made that choice in favor of demon, the great desolation. He had expressed the firm intention never to be buried in a cemetery—but why? Why did he not want a quiet cross over his body? Was he a confirmed pagan? What had he learned from that book he alone had read, whose ashes no one else would ever be able to decipher?

But death respected his wishes.

One day a short notice in the local paper said that in a patch of scrub known to the local people as the Horse Gates a boat had been found, and next to it the body of an unidentified man. It added that a double-barreled shotgun had been found beside the body. That year was a plague year and the gophers, those pretty little creatures of the steppe, were dying in great numbers. As a result the nomads were leaving their usual encampments and fleeing in terror, and since our hunter was already a week overdue on his usual rounds, some people who knew him sent out a search party; they were full of apprehension and foreboding. When the searchers returned they confirmed that the dead man was indeed the hunter. They reported the following story, which they had gotten from some fishermen.

For several nights they had been camping on a deserted island, and every night an unknown black dog came up, sat by their hut and howled softly. Neither beating nor shouts had any effect on her. They kept trying to chase her away, suspecting what her presence must mean, an unknown black dog on a deserted island. But she would invariably return the following night, with her eerie howling, disturbing the fishermen's slumbers.

At last a soft-hearted ranger went out after her: she yelped with joy and led him to an overturned boat: nearby, gun in hand, lay the body of a man completely picked over by birds; the only flesh remaining was in his boots. A cloud of birds circled above the body. A second dog, half dead, lay at his feet.

It was impossible to tell whether he had died of a fever, or whether it was the plague.

The waves beat steadily at the shoreline.

So he died as he had hoped; his strange desire was fulfilled. He ended his life far away from people.

His friends erected a little cross on his grave anyway. And that's how the wolf-killer died.

[pub. 1913]

K

I

I once had a Ka. Back in the days of White Kathay, Eve, as she stepped into a snowdrift from Andrée's air balloon, and a voice said "Go!" and she left in those Eskimo snows the print of her naked feet (don't you wish!)—Eve would have been astonished. To hear that word. But the people of Masr had heard it thousands of years before. And they were right when they split up the soul into the Ka, the Hu, and the Ba. Hu and Ba = man's reputation, good or bad. But the Ka is the soul's shadow, its double, its envoy to the world some snoring gentleman dreams of. There are no barriers for the Ka in time; he moves from dream to dream, breaks through time, and reaches the goal posts of bronze (the bronze of time).

He occupies the centuries as comfortably as he does a rocking chair. Consciousness does the same thing—it brings together moments of time like chairs in a living room.

My Ka was energetic, attractive, dark-skinned, gentle; he had huge feverish eyes, the eyes of a Byzantine god. His brow—a brow of Egypt—seemed to be made of small separate dots. Either we are savages, definitely, and the people of Masr were not—or the things Masr supplied for the soul were needful and natural, but somewhat extraneous.

And now—something about me.

I live in a city where signs say PUB IC BATHS, where you cannot escape the watchful eyes of sneaky savages who breed like rabbits and swarm in the trees. One savage, there, that woman—a silver fire flickers in her eyes, she walks in the plumes of a bird who was once alive, and another sneaky savage, a dead one, is already hunting it in the other world, a spear in his dead hand. Herds of fine-furred people browse the streets, and nowhere else does the thought of human stud farms come so easily to mind. "Otherwise, the human race is finished," they all think; and there I was, writing a book about human stud farms, while all around me these herds of fine-furred people moved.

I have a collection of friends—a little zoo, really, but I like them for their pedigree. I live on the third or fourth planet out, starting from the sun, and I try to think of the place as no more than, oh, a pair of gloves—something you always want handy to throw in the faces of the rabbit-people.

Is there anything more I can tell you? I foresee huge fights over whether to spell my name with an i or an e. I have no mammae on top, no maxillae on bottom. And no antennae. Height: shorter than an elephant, taller than an ant. Eyes: two. But enough about me, no?

K, my Ka, was my friend. I loved him for his birdlike disposition, his serenity, his wit. He was as comfortable as a raincoat. He taught me words you can see with (eyewords) and words you can do with (handwords).

And here are a few of the things he did.

2

One time we met people who held themselves together with buttons. Really. Their insides were accessible through a flap of skin, buttoned down by little round hornlike protuberances. Whenever they ate, a furnace of thoughts glowed through this flap. That's really true.

I stood on a great steel bridge and threw a coin into a river, a two-kopeck piece. "Someone should be worried about the science of the future," I said. "I wonder if maybe someday some underwater archeologist will come along and find my sacrifice to the river?"

And K introduced me to a scientist from the year 2222.

Ah! It was only a year after the first infant cry of the Superstate ASTSU. "Astsu!" the scientist said, glancing at the date on the coin. Back in those days people believed in space, they didn't think much about time. He commissioned me to write up a description of human beings. I filled in all the blanks and handed in the form. "Number of eyes, two," he read. "Number of hands, two; number of feet, two; fingers, ten; toes, ten. Fingers and toes combined, twenty."

He slipped a thin, gleaming skull-ring onto his shadowy finger. We discussed the advantages and disadvantages of that particular number. "These figures," he said, with a piercing look from his large, intelligent eyes, "do they ever change?"

"Those are the maximum figures," I answered. "Of course people do turn up from time to time with only one arm or one leg. And there will be a significant increase in such people every 317 years."

"And yet," he answered, "this gives us enough information to calculate the equation of their death." "Language," remarked the scientist from the year 2222, "is the everlasting source of knowledge. What is the relationship between gravity and time? It's perfectly clear that in your language the word *vremya,* which means time, and the word *ves,* which means weight, stand in the same relation as the word *bremya,* which means burden, and the word *bes,* which is a name for the Fiend, the Evil One. But can one who sweats beneath a burden behave like the Fiend? No. *Bremya* absorbs the force of *bes*. Where there are burdens to be borne, the Fiend is absent. In the same way, therefore, *vremya* absorbs the force of *ves,* for do we not abandon weight when we enter into time? The very soul of your language shows us that weight and time are different absorbtions of the same force."

He thought the whole thing over. "Yes," he said, "language contains more truths than we know."

At which point our acquaintance was broken off.

3

Another time K grabbed me by the arm and said, "Let's go see Amenhotpe." I saw Ay there, and Shurura, and Nafertiti. Shurura had a black beard, all curls.

"Hello there," said Amenhotpe. He nodded at us and then continued. "O Aton! Thus speaks your son Noferkheperura: Some gods swim and some gods fly, and some gods even crawl around on the ground. Sukh, for instance, and Mnevis, and

Bennu. In fact, is there a single mouse on the banks of Hapi-the-Nile who does not demand to be worshiped? All those gods quarrel among themselves, so a poor man is left with no god to pray to. He's happy if someone simply announces 'I am the One' and demands a fatted calf or two. By the Nine Bows and Arrows! Did you not tremble once, all of you, at the warcry of my ancestors?

"And if I am here, while Sheshat holds my shade in her resourceful hand, does not her hand preserve me-here from me-there? By the Nine Bows and Arrows! Isn't my Ka at this very moment among the clouds, lighting the blue Hapi-Nile with pillars of fire? I-here command you to adore me-there! And you, strangers, convey what I say to your own times."

K introduced him to the scientist from the year 2222.

Amenhotpe had a very weak body but very broad cheekbones, and the curve of his large eyes was graceful, childlike.

Another time I visited Akbar and Asoka. On the way back we got very tired.

We tried to stay clear of trains and kept hearing the drone of Sikorsky airplanes. We were hiding from both of them, and learned how to sleep and keep moving. Our heads were asleep, but our feet kept moving; they were an independent unit. I met this one artist and asked him if he was going to war. "I'm already at war," he answered, "only it's a war to conquer time, not space. I crouch in my trench and grab scraps of time from the past. It's a rough assignment, just as bad as you'd have in a battle for space." He always painted people with only one eye. I looked at his chokecherry eyes, his pale cheeks. K was walking beside us. It was pouring rain. This painter (Filonov) painted a feast of corpses, a feast of vengeance. The dead ate vegetables in a solemn ceremony, and over them all, like the rays of the moon, shone a grief-stricken madness.

Another time, on K's advice, I shaved my head all over, smeared myself red with cranberry juice, put a vial full of red ink in my mouth so I could spit it out if I had to; then I tied a belt around me, climbed into these mighty Moslem robes, put on a turban and lay down like I was dead. While I was doing that, K kept making war noises; he threw rocks at the mirror, banged on a tray, yelled like a wild man and shouted "Arrrrrrgh!"

And what do you think happened? Right away these two beautiful astonished houris showed up, with wonderful dark eyes and astonished eyebrows; they thought I was dead and picked me right up and carried me off someplace far away.

While they were greeting the faithful, they touched my brows tenderly with their lips, and that's how they cured my wounds. They probably noticed what flavor my blood was, but they were too polite to say anything. Three more houris came up laughing; they smudged their enchanting mouths in my ink and quickly wiped away my artificial wounds—total recovery of an imaginary invalid! From time to time the houris danced and their dark hair whirled behind them like blackbirds at play, or like the fleet of Syracuse after Alcibiades, just like little birds, one behind the other. It was a dance of joy.

It was a wreath of heads, which seemed to blur madly into a single stream. Later that joy died down a little, but still as before they looked at me with exultant eyes, with glittering nighttime eyes, and whispered among themselves. Mohammed came up and watched it all with a smile, and with a wicked gleam in his eyes. Lots of things today weren't real, he said. "But that's all right, young man, you just keep right on the way you're going. That's the spirit."

The next morning I woke up a bit tired: the houris were looking at me, slightly astonished, as if they'd just noticed something strange. Their mouths were scrubbed clean, clean, clean. And the red ink was gone from their hands. They looked as if they wanted to say something but couldn't make up their minds. But just at that moment I noticed a sign; on it was a message written in my own red ink. It said: "Unauthorized entry strictly prohibited." Beneath it was some complicated signature. I disappeared, but I remember the hair and the hands of the houris all messy with red ink, and lots more, and that very evening I sailed with the warriors of Vijaya to Sakhali, in the year 543 B.C. The houris appeared to me as they had done the night before, but now they wore veils made of dragonfly wings and fat coats made of forget-me-nots, rough and heavy, matted with the plants and their soil; they looked like deer covered with pale blue curls.

Now many of you I know are gamblers and have more than a nodding acquaintance with a deck of cards; some of you even have bad dreams involving sevens, aces, and ladies of hearts. But have any of you had the experience of gambling not with some specific individual, some John Doe, but with a collective of some kind—if only with the universal will? I have, it's a kind of game I'm very familiar with. I considered it much more fascinating than ordinary gambling, whose distinguishing features are candles, midnight, green tables, and scores scribbled in chalk. And I note, too, that your choice of moves is quite unlimited; if the game required it and you could somehow manage it, you could even take a damp sponge and wipe the constellations from the sky, like yesterday's lesson from a blackboard in school. But every gambler has to find his own moves for crushing his opponent.

You think of your opponent as your equal despite his universal nature, and the game proceeds upon a basis of mutual respect. And isn't that exactly what makes it so attractive? You feel that you know your opponent, and you become much more involved in the game than if you were betting against some ghost from the grave. K was my confidant, my intimate, in this pastime.

4

K sat sadly by the seashore, dangling his legs. Watch out, watch out! Jellylike sea creatures broken by the waves piled up at the shoreline, driven there by the wind in shifting dead shoals; they gleamed dully as they slipped from the fingers of women swimmers who seemed to be dark green, or even dark red, the fabrics they wore clung so close to their bodies. Some of them laughed with genuine delight when a wave caught them unawares. K was lean, muscular, and suntanned. He sat completely naked, except for a derby hat. His hair darkened by sea water hung to his shoulders. The dull sheen of the waves and the glitter at their crest were visible right through him. A seagull flew by beyond his gray form, and was visible through his shoulders though its colors faded at the moment of passage; as it flew on its black and white plumage brightened again. A woman in a green bathing suit with silver spots cut through him as she swam by. He flinched, then returned to his former outlines. She smiled boldly and glanced at him. K hunched his back. Meanwhile a figure that had been swimming for a long time left the water and came up onto the shore, water streamed from it like fur, it was a beast leaving the water. It threw itself onto the ground and lay still. K watched as two or three observant worms wrote the number six on the sand three times in succession, and then looked at one another significantly. A Tatar, a Moslem, was watering his black buffalos; they snapped their harnesses and rushed so far into the water only their dark eyes and their nostrils were visible above the surface; their bodies caked with filth and matted hair were completely submerged. He smiled suddenly, turned to a Christian fisherman, and said "al-Masih al-Dajjal." The fisherman knew what he meant, reached casually for his pipe, lit it, and casually remarked: "Who knows who he is. We're no experts . . . That's just something people say," he added. A man in military uniform who had been watching an occasional swimmer through a spyglass lowered it on the cord around his neck, glanced coldly at the fisherman, turned and walked off down a barely noticeable path.

But evening had fallen, and a flock of sea serpents swam through the water. The shore was deserted; only K remained sitting as he had been, arms folded over his knees. "Everything's boring," he thought, "Everything's finished." "Hey you! Shadow-hero!"—the voice seemed to come from the wind—"watch out!" But K didn't move. Then a wave washed him away, and up swam a great Beluga sturgeon who swallowed him whole. In this new destiny he became a round pebble and lived among seashells, a life preserver, and a piece of chain from a steamship. The Beluga had a weakness for old junk. It had also swallowed a belt with the name Fatima Menneda written in Arabic letters, dating from the days when the eagle of death rose up among spears, cutlasses, oars, and seaworms, and now death itself was reflected in the water, trailing blue earrings, laughing with sad eyes wide open once and for all, and with a splash of oars the barque sailed on, farther and farther, reflected in the nighttime water, and the feet of a white cloud brushed the deck like the feelers of a nighttime moth.

And then the mighty Beluga dies in the fisherman's nets.

5

And K was free again.

Gray-haired fishermen with their trousers rolled to the knee sang the Eddas, the sad song of the seacoast, and hauled on their nets—fragile, close-woven, dripping, hung here and there with dark crabs that clung to the mesh by their claws—straining their sinewy arms; sometimes they straightened up and stared at the eternal sea. Ospreys perched silently some distance away, like great guard dogs. The laughing lady of the sea sat on the stone that contained K, making wet footprints in the sand. The big fish now lay dead on the beach, glittering with the beetles that covered it.

But a girl found him and took him with her. Did she write a tanka on one side of him? "If death had your hair and your eyes, I would gladly die," and on the other side of the stone she paints a branch of ordinary green leaves; let them mark with their pattern the delicate surface of the flat white stone. The dark green pattern wrapped the rock in a net. He experienced the torments of Montezuma when everything became cloudless, or when Layla picked up the stone and put it to her lips and kissed it softly, unaware that it contained a living being, and spoke the Gogolian phrase "to one who knows how to smile." Iron Tolstoy was nearby, a delicate red seashell, very shiny and covered with dots, and wrinkled flowers with stone petals. Then K got bored and lonely and went to visit his master, who sang: "We ate En Sao, the spit of sick swallow, and we will eat, eat, eat it 'til the friends of En Sao." This indicated that he was angry.

"Oh," he said gloomily—"Well, let's hear what you have to say for yourself." He murmured the tale of his tribulations, "She was full of that unearthly, ineffable expression," and so on. What it amounted to was a list of complaints against destiny, its dark treasons, the nape of its neck.

K was ordered to return for sentry duty.

K saluted, touched his cap and disappeared, gray and winged.

The next morning he reported: "He's awake; I'm on guard duty here" (a rifle gleamed on his shoulders).

6

"Exclamation mark, question mark, three dots. The quarter the wind blows from, the wind of the gods, of the goddess Izanagi, of the fabric that covers her—snaky, half-silvered, ash gray. In order to understand her you must know that the ashen silver stripes alternate with transparent ones, like a window or an inkwell. The charm of this fabric can be fully grasped only when it is illuminated by the fitful fire of a joyful young arm. At such times a trace of fire runs across its waves of silver silk and then disappears, like wind over the grass. The fire of evening trembles on city buildings in the same way. Enormous, enchanting eyes. She calls herself adorable, enchanting . . ." "Wrong," I said, interrupting the flow of words. "You're wrong," I said severely. "Really?" K replied. His voice was sad, somewhat forced.

"Try to understand," he said a while later, cheering up a bit, as if he were announcing glad tidings: "Three mistakes: (1) in the city, (2) in the street, (3) in the house." But where exactly? "I don't know," K answered. His voice was vibrant with sincerity. Although I liked him a lot, we quarreled. He had to go away. He waved his wings, all dressed in gray, and disappeared. Twilight shivered at his feet, he looked like a leaping monk, my proud and beautiful wanderer. "Why that's him," several people exclaimed as they passed by; "he has such deep eyes." "But where is Tamara, where is Gudal?" Their fear of city people provided this opportunity of weaving these artistic fragments into the story. Meanwhile I walked up and down on the embankment, the wind ripped at my derby hat and blew sharp drops into my face and the dark cloth I wore. I watched the path of a cloud as it turned gold, and cracked my knuckles.

I knew K felt offended.

Once again he glimmered in the distance, occasionally waving his wings. It seemed to me then that I was a solitary singer and held the harp of blood in my hands. I was a shepherd: I had flocks of souls. Now he was gone. Meanwhile someone wrinkled and old came up to me. He looked around, glanced at me significantly, and said "It's coming! Soon!" nodded his head and disappeared. I followed him. We came to a grove of trees. Blackbirds and black-headed warblers hopped about in the foliage. Beautiful gray herons lowed and mooed like the hoarse-voiced cattle of the steppe, lifting their beaks high into heaven from the highest branch of a dried old oak. Then a hermit appeared, in a tall dry crumpled hat, all in black, among the oaks. His face was peevish and wrinkled. There was a hollow in one of the oaks; in it stood some icons and candles. The bark was gone from the tree, eaten up long ago by toothache sufferers. It was perpetual semi-twilight in the grove. Stag beetles scurried over the bark of the oak trees, duelling with one another, stabbing each other's wings. Between the black horns of one beetle you sometimes found the dried head of another. Made drunk by the sap of the oak trees, they were an easy prey for young boys. I fell asleep there, and "Layla and Majnun," the greatest story of the Aramaic peoples, once more inspired the dreams of a tired mortal. I was returning home and walked through a flock of fine-furred people. An exhibit of curiosities was on display in the city, and there I saw a stuffed monkey with foam on its black wax lips; the black stitching was clearly visible on its breast; in his arms he held a woman made of wax. I left.

This awful owl-fall, this strange and mysterious coincidence, astonished me. I believe that before a major war the word *pugovitsa* [button] has an especially frightening meaning, since the war—even though as yet undreamed of—lurks in that word like a conspirator, a harbinger lark, because the root of the word is related to *pugat'* [to frighten]. But among these overgrown brambles, these willows hung with thick rusty root-hairs, where everything was quiet and overcast, gray and uncompromising, where a solitary reveler tossed about in the air and the trees were severe and silent, some kind of dusty grass caught at my feet as if imploring me; it writhed on the ground like a sinner begging forgiveness. I kicked hard at the entangling grass, looked at it, and said "The common foot shall swell with power, and trample down the modest flower."

I was on my way home. They expected my coming and were waiting for me; they came out to meet me with their hands over their eyes. A tame viper, elegantly coiled, hung from my arm. I loved it.

"I have acted the part of the raven," I thought. "I have

brought the water of life, and then the water of death."

And I won't do it again!

7

K thought of that stone and the branch of ordinary gray-green leaves traced on it, and those words: "If death had curls and hair like yours, I would want to die," and flew into the blue expanse of the sky like a golden cloud among the crimson cloud peaks, steadily beating his wings, caught in a flock of red cranes, resembling, at that hour of early morning, the red ash of a fire-breathing mountain, and he too was red as they were, and tied by red threads, by swirls and filaments, to the fiery dawn.

The journey had been a long one, and drops of sweat, reddened now by the rays of dawn, gleamed on K's dark face. And then the mighty crane-trumpet of his warlike ancestors began to sound from somewhere high beyond the chalky white masses.

K folded his wings and landed on the earth, dripping head to foot with morning dew. From each feather hung a pearl of dew, coarse and black. No one noticed that he had landed somewhere near the source of the Blue Nile. He shook himself and beat the air three times with his wings like a swan in the moonlight. There was no going back to the past. Friends, fame, glory—all lay ahead. K climbed onto a wild horse, it was a mean one that had never been broken before, with golden stripes, and K let him nibble his shadowy but still beautiful knees as they galloped across the field. A pack of striped and bristling wolves pursued him with their high-pitched cries. Something in their voices reminded him of those who review young and gifted writers in the daily press and the periodicals. But the golden steed bent his head stubbornly and bit K's shadowy elbow; he was wild as ever. The fierce gallop exhilarated him. Two or three Nyam-nyams shot poison arrows at him, and then fell to the ground in superstitious terror.

He saluted the earth with a flourish of his hand. He stopped by a waterfall. Here he joined a company of apes lounging with a certain sophisticated nonchalance upon the roots and branches of trees. Some held infants in their pudgy hands and nursed them; young adolescents chattered as they swung through the trees. Black coats, powerful low skulls, and curved canines—all gave a fierce look to the hairy folk that made up the company. Cries of raucous delight rang through the twilight as evening approached. K joined their circle.

"In the old days," began a venerable old male with a calloused face, "things were very different."

"The Roc bird has vanished completely nowadays. Where has it gone? We do not fight with Hanno as we once did; once we grabbed away their swords and smashed them across our knees like rotten sticks, and covered ourselves with glory. He has gone away across the sea. And the Roc bird? No way now to wrap myself up in one of its great feathers, and then to lie down to sleep upon another!

"Long ago it used to wing its way down from the snowy mountains, its cry would wake the elephants each morning. And we used to say to ourselves: 'Listen! The Roc bird!' And in those days it would carry off baby elephants, up beyond the clouds; they would look down at earth, and their trunks would hang beneath the clouds and so would their legs, but their eyes and their gray foreheads and their ears would all poke out on top, above the blue edges of the clouds.

"And now the bird is gone! Farewell, Roc bird! . . ."

And all the apes rose from their seats and cried out together, "Farewell!"

Not far away next to a fire sat the White One; she was wrapped in the remains of a shawl. She was clearly the one who had lit the fire, and on the strength of this accomplishment they accorded her a certain respect. The old ape addressed her.

"White One," he said, "when you were crossing the desert, we knew, and we sent out our young braves to find you, and now you are one of us, even though many looked their last upon the stars. Sing us a song in your native tongue."

White One stood up. She was very young. She glanced at an elderly ape sitting by the path. "Move, grandma," she said, and she shook out her golden hair; it enveloped her in a luxuriant golden haze.

Her hair made a soft murmur, it descended like water on

fire over her shoulders, and they blushed hot and cold. An exquisite sorrow was expressed in her movements. She was strikingly beautiful as well, with a perfect body. K noticed that a toenail on her wonderfully proportioned foot reflected the whole of the clearing in the forest, the gathering of apes, the smoking fire, and a patch of sky. It was a minuscule mirror where you could see the elders of the tribe, their hairy bodies, the tiny young ones, the entire tribe of forest dwellers. Their faces seemed to be expecting the end of the world and the advent of someone.

Their features were twisted with grief and anger; a low wail escaped their lips from time to time. K set an elephant tusk on end and at the top, as if they were pegs for strings, he fastened years: 411, 709, 1237, 1453, 1871; and below on the footboard the years 1491, 1193, 665, 449, 31. Strings joined the upper and the lower pegs; they vibrated faintly.

"Will you sing something?" he asked.

"Yes," she said. She placed her fingers on the strings and began:

> "By the will of the envious fates I stand among you;
> If the fates were artless dressmakers merely
> I would tell them they used their needle badly,
> I would never accept their designs,
> I would sit down myself at their benches.
> Steel itself beneath our hands
> Will sing 'Uthlofan, laufling!' "

She moved her hand across the strings; they sounded the thunder-boom of a flock of swans that settles as one body onto a lake.

K observed that each string consisted of six parts, each part consisting of 317 years, 1902 years in all. And also that the top row of pegs indicated years when the East attacked the West, while the pegs at the lower end of the strings indicated an opposite movement, the West against the East. In the top row were the Vandals, Arabs, Tatars, Turks, and Germans; below were the Egyptians of Hatshepsut, the Greeks of Odysseus, the Scythians, the Greeks of Pericles, the Romans. K attached one additional string: between the year 78, the invasion of the Scythians of

Adia Saka, and the year 1980—the East. K studied the possibilities of playing on all seven strings.

Meanwhile Layla wept bitterly, her beautiful blonde hair trailing on the ground.

"You do your duty badly, you use your needle bitterly," she said, and sobbed bitterly. K broke his branch and placed it beside the weeping girl.

Layla gave a start and said:

"Once in my tranquil childhood days
I had a rounded pebble,
And on it was a branch like this."

K moved away into the twilight; suppressed sobs choked him; he dried his tears on green leaves and remembered a white-painted dormer, flowers, books.

"Listen," the old one said, "and I will tell you of she who came as a guest among the apes. She came to visit us once, riding upon a moa. A dead butterfly, impaled on a porcupine quill and thrust into her black hair, took the place of her fan, and she fanned herself with it. In her hand was a willow twig with silvery buds, the hand of the Venus of the Apes; she clutched the moa, with her black palm she held onto its wings, to its breast. Her face was raven black, and curly black hair covered her softly like the fleece of night. She had an attractive, passionate smile. We thought of her as our little lamb. She laughed as she made her way across our land. She was our goddess of black breasts, our goddess of nocturnal sighs."

Layla: "If death had hair and curls like yours, I would want to die." She walked off into the twilight, arms clasped above her head.

"But where is Amenhotpe?" voices questioned. K realized someone was missing. "Who?" he asked. "Amenhotpe, son of Tiye," they replied with particular deference. "We believe that he walks here by the waterfall, repeating the name Nafertiti."

Ay, Tutu, Aziri, and Shurura, keeper of the sword, all stood around. But before the migration of souls our sovereign had been the sovereign of the muddy Hapi-Nile. And Ankhsenpaaton walks through Hut Aton to Hapi to pick flowers. Isn't that what he dreams of now?

And now Amenhotpe arrives. The ape people fall silent; they rise. "Be seated," said Amenhotpe, as he stretched out his hand. Deep in meditation, he lowered himself to the ground. Everyone sat down. The fire flared up and, gathered beside it, four Ka's spoke about themselves: the Ka of Akhenaton, the Ka of Akbar, the Ka of Asoka, and K. The word "superstate" was mentioned more often than it should have been. We whispered among ourselves. But a terrible uproar threw us into confusion; white men rushed in and attacked us like wild animals. A shot. Bullets whistled overhead. "Amenhotpe is wounded, Amenhotpe is dying!" Word spread quickly through the ranks of our warriors. It became a rout, a disaster. Many individuals died bravely, but all in vain. "Go, carry my spirit to him most worthy to receive it!" said Akhenaton to his Ka as he closed his eyes. "Give him my kiss. Save yourselves! Run for your lives!"

The four spirits flew for a long time through the threatening ash-smoke sky; they carried the White One, who had fallen into a deep swoon, her golden hair trailing behind her. Only once did a moth raise its head, while in an estuary a seahorse snorted. The escape was successful; no one saw them.

8

But what actually happened in that forest? How was Amenhotpe killed?

I. Amenhotpe the son of Tiye

1. I am Akhenaton.
2. The son of Amun.
3. What says Ay, father of the gods?
4. Will you not grant me a *shawabty*?
5. I am the god of gods; thus did *rometu* glorify me; and I hereby let you go, as if you were ordinary workers—Osiris, Hathor, Sobek, all of you. I have demoted you, like a *rabisu*. O sun, Ra Aton.
6. Ay, let us create words a plowman can understand. You priests, you are nothing but a cloud of gnats swarming

by the stone reeds of the temples! In the beginning was the word . . .

7. O Nafertiti, help me!
   I have inundated all the fields of Hapi,
   I have brought you unto the Sun, you *rometu,*
   I will carve into the stone of walls
   That I am Akhenaton, godfather of the sun.
   I have brushed away the clouds of superstition
   from the shining face of Ra.
   And in a quiet whisper the *shawabty*
   repeats after me: You are right!
   O Akhenaton, narrow-chested godfather of the sun!
8. Now grant me the turtle's shield. And your sounding strings, Ay! Is there a single mouse by Hapi to whom they would not erect a temple? They grunt, they moo, they roar; they chomp hay, they catch beetles and devour slaves. Entire holy cities grow up around them. There are more gods than there are nongods. The situation is chaotic.

II. Amenhotpe the Black Ape
(striped wolfcubs, a parrot)

1. Haoo-haoo.
2. Zhrabr chap-chap!
3. Oogoom mkhee! Mkhee!
4. bgaf! gkhaf ha! ha! ha!
5. Ebza cheetoren! Epssi kai-kai! (He wanders in a shadowy oak grove and picks flowers.) Mgooom map! Map! Map! Map! (He eats little baby birds.)
6. Meeo bpeg! Viig.
   Ga kha! Mal! bgkhaf! gkhaf!
7. Egzheezeoo ravira!
   Mal! Mal! Mal! Mai, mai. Khaeeo khao kheeootseeoo.
8. r-r-r-ra ga-ga. Ga! graf! Ennma meh-eh-eeoo-ooeeai!

Amenhotpe, in a utang-skin, lives through the day he spent yesterday. He eats an arboreal vegetable, plays on a lute made from the skull of a baby elephant. The others listen. A tame Russian parrot speaks:

"A transparent sky. The stars are shining. Did you hear? Have you seen? A singer of his own love, a singer of his own sorrow."

The voices of elephants trumpet as they return from the watering hole.

A Russian hut in the forests near the Nile.

The arrival of the white man, the animal trader.

The log walls are covered with guns, antlers, the works of Chekhov. A baby elephant with an iron chain on its leg.

Trader Plumes, tusks: very good, my fren'. An order for an ape: one full-grown male.

You understan'? No need live one, dead ok, for stuffed one; sew up sides, make wax foam on mouth, little wax figure like fainting person in arms. From town to town. Tee-hee! I come here: frisky female, very young, she scurry over rocks with water jar. Knock-knock-knock! Little feet. Real cheap. Another glass wine, my fren'.

Old One Listen to me, esteemed master. He will become angry, and may disturb my esteemed master's combed hair, perhaps even rumple his collar.

Trader Just say goodbye. Don't get mad. Hee-hee! So tomorrow, we hunt? Get your guns ready, natives for ambush. She comes with jar to get water, he comes out, gets killed. Aim for the forehead and black chest.

Woman with the Water Jar I feel sorry for you; you will peep out from behind a pinetree and just at that moment a well-aimed shot will bring your death. And from what I heard, you aren't an ordinary monkey, either, you are Akhenaton. Here he is! I will look at you lovingly, to brighten your dying moments with the autumn of desire. My dear, my terrifying admirer. Smoke! A shot! A terrible cry!

[*Amenhotpe*] *the Black Ape* Meh-oo! Manch! Manch! Manch! *(He falls, tries to stop the bleeding wound with dried grass.)*

Voices We got him! He's dead! Dance! Prepare a feast for tonight!

(The woman places her hand on his forehead.)

Amenhotpe Manch! Manch! Manch! *(He dies. The spirits pick up Layla and carry her off.)*

(Ancient Egypt; the priests are plotting revenge.)

He has trampled our customs and makes all men equal in the world of the dead; he has shaken our foundations . . . Death! Death!

(The priests hop about with their arms raised to heaven.)

Akhenaton Oh, the fifth evening, let loose the mooring line! Sail out "the grandeur of love" and move the oars as if they were eyelashes. Hathor weeps tenderly, lovingly, she laments her lovely Horus.

The cow face . . . the calf horns . . . the broad torso. The massive thrust above the waist.

And the tumbled shadow of Hathor with its cow's horns, that the moon silvers in the depths of Hapi, was cut by an agile pangolin with its armored saw. It was joined by another; they snarled over the body of a slave.

Face down, beautiful, dead, he floated down upon Hapi.

Priests (softly) Poison. Hey, Akhenaton, drink this. The day is hot. He drank it! *(They leap up.)* He is dead!

Akhenaton (as he falls) Shurura, where are you? Ay, where are the incantations? Oh, Nafertiti, Nafertiti! *(He falls; foam appears on his lips. He dies, clutching the air with his hand.)*

And that is what happened by the waterfall.

9

All this happened back in the days when people made the first flights over the capital city of the north. I lived high then, and thought about the seven measured feet of time. Egypt, then Rome, Russia alone, England; I drifted from the dust of Copernicus to the dust of Mendeleev, constantly aware of the noise of a Sikorsky airplane. I was preoccupied by the wavelengths of good and evil, I dreamed of the convexo-convex lenses of good and evil, because I knew that black burning rays coincided with knowledge of evil, and cold bright rays with knowledge of good. I thought about bits of time melting into the universe, and about death.

To the frozen path between stars
I shall not fly with a prayer,
I shall fly there dead, cold,
With a razor covered with blood.

There are the violins of a tremulous throat, one still youthful, and of a cold razor. There is the luxurious landscape of my darkening blood on the petals of white flowers. One friend of mine—you remember him—died that way; he thought like a lion, but died like a lamb. A friend came to see me, a friend with dark eyes, a joyful savagery shone in them—with dark eyes and a girlfriend. They brought me wreaths and bouquets, armfuls of the hay of fame. I looked like the Yenisei in winter. They fed me like the ravens. They were so boldly amorous, they even embraced in my presence, and paid no attention to the hidden lion, the baby mice!

They went off to Didova Khata. On the crumpled dry petal of a lotus I sketched a head of Amenhotpe; a lotus from the mouth of the Volga, or Ra.

Suddenly, in the nighttime window that looked out into Kamenoostrovsky Boulevard, the glass shattered, it fell everywhere, and through that window appeared the head of Layla, lying peacefully stretched out like a box of vegetables. She seemed dead. At that moment the four Ka's came into my room. They brought me the sad tidings: "Akhenaton is dead. We have brought you his testament." He handed me a letter sealed with the black resin of the abracadasp. A young boa constrictor wound itself in coils about my arm; I put him down and felt Layla's soft arms around my neck.

The boa raised itself in a curve and looked at us coldly, evilly, with unmoving eyes. She tightened her arms joyfully around my neck (perhaps I was the prolongation of her dream) and spoke only one word: "Majnun."

The Ka's moved aside, deeply touched, and wiped their tears in silence. They wore fieldboots and buckskin trousers. They wept. In the name of his friends my Ka gave me a kiss from Amenhotpe, and the kiss smelled of gunpowder. We were sitting beside a silver samovar and its silver curve (or at least it seemed silver to me) reflected me, Layla, and the four Ka's: mine, Vijaya, Asoka, and Amenhotpe.

[March 7–March 23, 1915]

October on the Neva

My birthday. Sinister thunder over Tsarskoe Selo. Every night on my way home I used to walk through the city of the insane and I always used to think of someone I knew in the army, Private Lysak, he was crazy and kept whispering over and over: "Truth, no truth; truth, no truth."

His quickening whisper would keep getting faster and faster and softer and softer, and then the poor guy would jump into bed and hide under the covers, pull them up until only his eyes were showing, as if he wanted to get away from someone, but he never stopped that inhumanly fast whisper. Then, very slowly, he would sit up in bed and his whisper would get louder and louder and he would squat there absolutely rigid, his eyes round as a hawk's and all yellow, and then all of a sudden he would straighten up and start shaking his bed and yelling "TRUTH," screaming like crazy so that the whole building echoed and the windows rattled.

"Where is truth?" he shouted. "Bring me the truth! Bring it here!"

Then he sat down. He had a long wiry moustache and yellow eyes, and he would sit there trying to catch sparks from the fire with his bare hands, only there wasn't any fire. By that time the attendants would come running from all over. It was like notes from the field of the dead, flickers of heat lightning over the distant field of death, a sign at the dawn of the century. He was a big powerful man, and he looked like a prophet in his hospital bed.

We all used to meet in Petrograd—me, Petnikov, Petrovsky, Lurie, sometimes Ivnev would be there and some of the other Presidents.

"The point is, friends, we weren't wrong when we said we thought the monster of war had only one eye left, and all we had to do was char the end of a log, sharpen it to a point, and ram it as hard as we could into that eye, blind him with it, and then hide ourselves in the fleece. Am I right when I say that? Am I telling the truth?"

"Absolutely right," we answered. So we decided to put out the one eye of war. The Government of Planet Earth published a little list: "Signatures of the Presidents of Planet Earth" on a blank page, nothing else. That was our first step.

"You dead must return and join us in the struggle! The living are worn out," somebody shouted out loud. "We want to be a single host of warriors, the dead and the living together. Rise up, you dead men! Leave your graves!"

In those days the word *bolshevik* was frequently spoken with a strange pride, and it was soon clear that gunfire was about to blaze through the twilight of "today."

Petrovsky, with his enormous Caucasian fur hat, his transparent, emaciated face, would smile mysteriously.

"You hear that?" he used to ask, when a drainspout would gurgle suddenly as we passed.

"Whatever just went on in there, I'll never make sense of it," he announced, and began beating on the pipe mysteriously; his look said clearly that things would keep on going wrong.

He was in a sinister mood.

Later on, just before Kerensky's downfall, I heard an astonished remark: "He's been in for nine months now, and he's so entrenched it will take cannons to get him out."

What was he waiting for? Was there anyone left who didn't think he's a pathetic laughingstock?

The Provisional Government was meeting in the Mariinsky Palace at that time, and one day we sent them the following letter:

To the Provisional Government, Mariinsky Palace, City

Attention Everybody!

The Government of Planet Earth at its meeting on October 22 has decided:

1. To consider the Provisional Government provisionally

nonexistent, and the Head Improviser Alexander Fedorovich Kerensky under close arrest.

"Heavy is the grip of the handshake of stone."

Presidents of Planet Earth: Petnikov, Ivnev, Lurie, Petrovsky. Me-the-statue-of-the-Commendatore.

Another time we sent the following letter:

To Alexandra Fedorovna Kerenskaia, Winter Palace, City

Attention Everybody!
Are you really still not aware that the Government of Planet Earth already exists? Yes, you are really still not aware that it already exists.

The Government of Planet Earth (signed)

One time we were all together and champing at the bit, so we decided to telephone the Winter Palace.

"Winter Palace? Operator, please connect us with the Winter Palace."

"Hello, Winter Palace? This is the Moving-Van Workers' Cooperative."

"Yes, what can I do for you?" The voice was cold, polite, humorless.

"The moving-van workers would like to know how soon the occupants of the Winter Palace will be moving out."

"What? What?"

"Are the residents of the Winter Palace planning to move?"

"Ah! And is that all you want to know?" We could hear a sour smile in the voice.

"That's all." We could hear someone laughing at the other end of the line. Petnikov and I began laughing on our end.

A look of dismay on the face of someone in the next room.

Two days later the cannons began firing.

Don Giovanni was playing at the Mariinsky that week, and for some reason we identified Kerensky with the Don; I remember how everybody in the opposite row of boxes winced and looked suspicious when one of us nodded his head, agreeing to the Don's invitation before the Commendatore managed to do so.

A few days later the *Aurora* rode silently at anchor on the Neva across from the Palace, and the long cannon that had been installed on her deck looked like an unblinking eye of iron—a sea monster's eye.

The story was that Kerensky had escaped wearing a Red Cross nurse's uniform and that he had been bravely defended by his last line of defense, the Girl Scouts of Petrograd.

Nevsky Prospect was full of people, constantly crowded, and there was no shooting there whatsoever. There were bonfires by all the raised bridges, guarded by sentries in heavy sheepskin coats with their rifles stacked, while densely packed formations of sailors in black moved silently from place to place, inseparable elements of the night itself. All you could make out was the rhythmic movement of pleats in their uniforms. By morning we found out that all the military academies had been taken over, one after the other. But the inhabitants of the capital were not involved in the struggle.

The situation in Moscow was entirely different; there the fighting was serious: we were holed up for a week. We spent the nights on Kazansky sitting at a table with our heads on our arms; during the day we came under fire on Trubnaia and Miasnitskaia streets.

Other parts of the city were completely cordoned off. Still, once I walked around Moscow on the Sadovaia late at night, even though I was stopped and searched a couple of times.

The pitch dark was occasionally broken by passing armored cars; from time to time I heard shots.

And finally there was a truce.

We rushed outside. The cannons were silent. We ran through the hungry streets like kids after the first snowfall, looking at the frosty stars of bullet holes in windows, at the snowy flowers of tiny cracks; we walked through the shards of glass, clear as ice, that covered Tverskoy Boulevard. Pleasant, those first hours, when we picked up bullets that had smashed against walls, all bent and twisted, like the bodies of burnt-up butterflies.

We saw the black wounds of smoking walls.

In one store we saw a big gray cat; she meowed through the plate glass, trying to entice people into letting her out; but she remained in her solitary confinement for a long time.

We wanted to name everything after ourselves. In spite of the angry barrage of iron fired from Sparrow Hills, the city was whole.

I especially loved the south embankment of the Moscow River, with its three factory chimneys that looked like candles lit there by some determined hand, its cast-iron bridge and the crows that gathered on the ice. But over it all like golden onion domes towered the candelabrum of the three factory chimneys, held there by some enormous hand. An iron staircase led to their summits, and sometimes a man would climb to the top, a priest like a candle that burned before a face made of gray factory soot.

Whose face was it? Friend or foe? A forehead outlined by smoke, hanging over the city, wound with a beard of clouds? Or was it perhaps a new Qurrat al-Ain, dark-eyed, consecrating her wonderful silken hair to the flames that consume her, prophesying equality and equal rights? As yet we did not know. We could only look.

But these new candles now burn for an unknown hierarch, and they dominate the old sanctuary.

It was here too that I first looked into the book of the dead, when I saw the line of people by Lomonosov Park, a long line that filled the entire street by the entrance to the morgue; they were relatives come to claim their dead.

The initial letter of a new age of freedom is often written with the ink of death.

[1918]

Vladimir Mayakovsky, drawing of Khlebnikov, 1916

Projects for the Future

Khlebnikov, drawing of Vladimir Tatlin, ca. 1915

Human beings have long perceived the workings of destiny—the grand pattern of the mover of the universe—in coincidence, in accident, in the moment of perception of a problem previously unsuspected. So did Khlebnikov. Destiny was his prime concern. The category of those who study the workings of the universe is unclear—Lucretius and Dante may be scientists, just as Newton and Einstein may be poets. Khlebnikov was both. For him, the shift in sound that produces a shift in meaning was a shift in the structure of the universe. That the shift of a vowel made the Russian word for sword (*mech*) become the word for ball (*miach*) gave Khlebnikov a vertiginous sense of the power of language to influence the natural world. The shift of a consonant was all that distinguished *inventors* from *investors* or *explorers* from *exploiters*—and suddenly there appears the image of a struggle between *N* and *S*, between *R* and *T*. The movement of consonants became a metaphor for political and economic conflict.

To many of his readers this seemed, and seems, like nonsense. But we must be careful to distinguish, as he did, between nonsense and *beyonsense* (*zaum*, in Russian). The word *zaum* was part of the Futurist vocabulary, used by different poets in different ways. In Khlebnikov the word must be seen first as a function of its root, the word *um*: intellect, intelligence, reason, the rational faculty of the mind. *Um* implies the creation of "pilings," the foundations of the man-made structures that must sooner or later destroy the mind's unity with the natural world. *Um* also implies the separation of thinking man from the natural stuff of language: the shape, sound, and color of words. The opposite of *um* is magic, magic words, the part of language that contains a power inaccessible to the intellect and is always opposed to it. It is here that poetry stands—but poetry had been weakened during the nineteenth century, especially in Russia, by positivism and historicism. So Khlebnikov attempts a radical *corrective: to reclaim a power for poetry by reaching back beyond* (za) *intellect* (um), *to the roots of language.*

The "strange wisdom" of language perceived in this way, he writes below in the fragmentary essay "On Poetry," "may be broken down into truths contained in separate sounds: sh, m, v, *etc. We do not yet understand these sounds. We confess that honestly. But there is no doubt that these sound sequences constitute a series of universal truths passing before the predawn of our soul." The purpose of beyonsense is to return to poetry a status as life-sustaining communication, relieved of worn-out words, those "clumps of intellect, stacks of sense,/a wagon train of dead ideas." Beyonsense was to make language ready for the future.*

The tone of some of the pieces that follow is aggressive, polemical, aimed at the established older generation of Symbolist writers—Briusov, Balmont, Merezhkovsky—and their journal Libra. *It is the tone of an impatient young man, aware of his Russianness and concerned to defend it against Western influences. "!Futurian!" attacks the wave of European influence that Symbolism represented in Russia. "The Word as Such" defends Russian Futurism from the prior claims of Italian Futurism. In "The Trumpet of the Martians" and "An Appeal by the Presidents of Planet Earth," the voice of the younger generation makes a more sweeping claim: in 1916 Khlebnikov with his friend and disciple Grigory Petnikov founded the Society of 317, intended to be an association of creative scientists, writers, and thinkers from various countries who would form a world government and oppose the evils wrought by political states. Soon Khlebnikov's name for himself and his group of friends evolved into the Presidents of Planet Earth, "inventor/explorers" who took a stand against the "investor/exploiters" of this world.*

The most astonishing of these pieces are the visions of the future, where Khlebnikov predicts some of modern technology's most compelling achievements. His essay "The Radio of the Future" foresees the global communication network of present-day television, while "Ourselves and Our Buildings" and "A Cliff Out of the Future" describe with accuracy and a certain amount of wit the wonders of late twentieth-century urban architecture and city planning. "To the Artists of the World" envisages a universal written language.

All these projects are universal in scope, and they aim at the same restructuring of the world as did the 1917 Revolution—which, we must always remember, echos at the margins of all these texts. But Khlebnikov's projects attempt to set humanity free from the tyranny of history and causality; they could not compete with an ideology organized on those very premises.

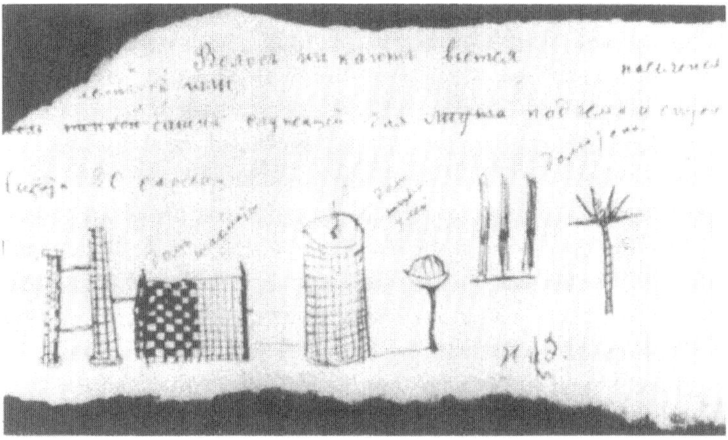

Khlebnikov, architectural sketches, ca. 1919

"Let them read on my gravestone"

Let them read on my gravestone: He wrestled with the notion of species and freed himself from its hold. He saw no distinction between human and animal species and stood for the extension to the noble animal species of the commandment and its directive: "Love thy neighbor as thyself." He called the indivisible noble animal species his "neighbors," and would point out the advantage of utilizing experiences from the past life of the most ancient species. So he supposed that it would benefit the human race to introduce into human behavior something like the system of worker bees in a hive, and he often emphasized that he saw in the concept of worker bees his own personal ideal. He raised high the banner of Galilean love, and the shadow of that banner fell on many a noble animal species. The heart, the real meat of the contemporary impulse forward of human societies, he saw not in the princely individual, but in the prince-tissue: the princely lump of human tissue confined in the calcium box of the skull. He was inspired to dream of being a prophet and a great interpreter of the prince-tissue, and of that alone. Divining its will, with a single impulse of his own flesh, blood, and bone, he dreamed of increasing the ratio ϵ/ρ, where ϵ equals the mass of prince-tissue and ρ equals the mass of peasant-tissue, as far as he personally was concerned. He dreamed of the distant future, of the earthball of the future, and his dreams were inspired when he compared the earth to a little animal of the steppe, darting from bush to bush. He discovered the true classification of the sciences, he linked time and space, he established a geometry of numbers. He discovered the Slav principle. He founded an institute for the study of the prenatal life of the child. He discovered the microbe that causes progressive paralysis. He linked and explained the fundamentals of chemistry in space. Enough, let a page be devoted to him, and indeed not one alone.

He was such a child he imagined that six came after five, and seven after six. He used even to dare think that as a general rule wherever we have one and then one more, we also have three, and five, and seven, and infinity—∞.

Of course, he never thrust his opinion on anyone else, he considered it belonged to him personally, and he recognized that the most sacred and holiest of all rights was to be able to hold a contrary opinion.

On the five-and-more senses.

Five aspects, there are five of them, but that's not enough. Why not simply say: there is only one, but a great one?

Pattern of points, when will you fill up the white spaces, when will you populate the vacant slots?

There is a certain muchness, a manifold with an unspecified number of dimensions incessantly altering its shape, which in relation to our five senses stands in the same position as a continuous two-dimensional space stands in relation to a triangle, a circle, an ovoid, a rectangle.

That is, just as a triangle, a circle, an octagon are parts of a plane, so our senses of hearing, seeing, taste, and smell are parts, accidental lapses of this one great, extended manifold.

It has raised its lion's head and looks at us, but its mouth is sealed.

Furthermore, just as by the continuous alteration of a circle one may obtain a triangle, and the triangle may be continually altered to form an octagon, and just as from a sphere in three-dimensional space through continuous variation one can obtain an egg, an apple, a horn, a barrel, just so there exist certain quantities, independent variables, which as they change transform the senses of the various classes—for example, sound and sight or smell—one into the other.

Thus by changing certain existing values, the blue color of a cornflower (I mean the pure sensation as such) can be continuously varied through areas of disjunction we humans are unaware of and be transformed into the sound of a cuckoo's call or a child's crying; it *becomes* them.

During this process of continuous variation, it forms a certain one-dimensional manifold, all of whose points, except those close to the first and last, belong to a region of unknown sensations, as if they come from another world.

Surely such a manifold has at least once illuminated the mind of a dying man, flashing like a lightning bolt that links two swollen clouds, linking two orders of experience in the inflamed consciousness of a diseased brain.

Perhaps at the moment just before death, when all is haste, when everything in fear and panic abandons itself to flight, rushes headlong, leaps all barriers, abandons hope of saving the whole, the sum total of many personal lives, and is concerned for itself alone, when what happens in a man's head resembles what happens in a city inundated by hungry waves of molten lava, perhaps at that moment just before death in a terrifying rush in every human head there occurs just such a filling up of gaps and ditches, such destruction of forms and fixed boundaries. And perhaps in every human consciousness, in just such a terrifying rush, a sensation that belongs to one order, *A,* is transformed into a sensation of a different order, *B,* and only then, after it has become *B,* does that sensation slow down and become graspable, the way we can distinguish the spokes of a wheel only when the speed of its revolution drops below a certain limit. The speeds at which the sensations move across that unknown space are selected in such a way that the sensations most closely connected, positively or negatively, with the safety of the whole being move most slowly, and may thus be examined with precision, in the greatest detail. Those sensations which have the least to do with matters of survival pass more rapidly and the consciousness is unable to dwell upon them.

[December 7, 1904]

The Word as Such

In 1908 we were preparing materials for *A Jam for Judges I;* some of it wound up in that book, some of it in *The Impressionists' Studio.* In both books V. Khlebnikov, the Burliuks, S. Miasoedov, and others indicated a new path for art: the word was developed as itself alone.

Henceforth a work of art could consist of a *single word,* and simply by a skillful alteration of that word the fullness and expressivity of artistic form might be attained.

But this is an expressivity of another kind. The work of art was both perceived and criticized (at least they had some premonition of this) merely as a word.

A work of art is the art of the word.

From which it followed automatically that tendentiousness and literary pretensions of any kind were to be expelled from works of art.

Our approximation was the machine—impassive, passionate.

The Italians caught a whiff of these Russian ideas and began to copy from us like schoolboys, making imitation art.

They had absolutely no sense of verbal matters before 1912 (when their big collection came out), and none after.

But of course the Italians had started with tendentiousness. Like Pushkin's little devil, they sang their own praises and claimed responsibility for everything contemporary, when what was called for was not sermonizing about it but to leap onto the back of the contemporary age and ride off full speed, to offer it as the grand summation of all their work.

After all, a sermon that doesn't derive from the art itself is nothing but wood painted to look like metal. And who would trust a weapon like that? These Italians have turned out to be noisy self-promotors, but inarticulate pipsqueaks as artists.

They ask us about our ideal, about emotional content? We

rule out both destructiveness and accomplishment, we are neither fanatics nor monks—all Talmuds are equally destructive for the word-worker; he remains face to face, always and ultimately, with the word (itself) alone.

A. Kruchonykh
V. Khlebnikov
[1913]

The Letter as Such

No one argues any more about the word as such, they even agree with us. But their agreement does no good at all, because all those who are so busy talking after the fact about the word say nothing about the letter. They were all born blind!

The word is still not valued, the word is still merely tolerated.

Why don't they just go ahead and dress it up in gray prison clothes? You've seen the letters of their words—strung out in straight lines with shaved heads, resentful, each one just like all the others—gray, colorless—not letters at all, just stamped-out marks. And yet if you ask a write-wright, a real writer, he'll tell you that a word written in one particular handwriting or set in a particular typeface is totally distinct from the same word in different lettering.

You certainly wouldn't dress up all your lady friends in standard issue overalls! Damn right you wouldn't, they'd spit in your face if you did. But not the word—the word can't say a thing. Because it is dead—martyred like Boris and Gleb. Your words are all born dead.

You're worse than Sviatopolk the martyr-maker!

Two circumstances obtain:

1. Our mood alters our handwriting as we write.

2. Our handwriting, distinctively altered by our mood, conveys that mood to the reader independently of the words. We must therefore consider the question of written signs—visible, or simply palpable, that a blind man could touch. It's clearly not necessary that the author himself should be the one who writes a handwritten book; indeed, it would probably be better for him to entrust the task to an artist. But until today there have been no such books. The first ones have now been issued by the Futurians, for example: *Old-Time Love,* copied over for printing by

Mikhail Larionov; *Blow-Up,* by Nikolai Kulbin and others; *A Duck's Nest,* by Olga Rozanova. About these books it is finally possible to say: every letter is letter perfect.

It's strange that neither Balmont nor Blok—to say nothing of those who would seem to be the most up to date of our contemporaries—has ever thought of giving his offspring to an artist instead of a typesetter.

When a piece is copied over, by someone else or even by the author himself, that person must reexperience himself during the act of recopying, otherwise the piece loses all the rightful magic that was conferred upon it by handwriting at the moment of its creation, in the "wild storm of inspiration."

V. Khlebnikov
A. Kruchonykh

[1913]

!Futurian!

We rang for room service and the year 1913 answered: it gave Planet Earth a valiant new race of people, the heroic Futurians. The Fathers (Briusov, Baby Balmont, Merezhkovsky, Tolstoy, and the rest), with napkins draped over their arms, served us another Tsushima on a platter.

The youn-n-n-ger generation has smashed the dish; a casual kick sent it flying from the hands of the panicky waiter.

We rang for *fresh* meat! Hungry younglings. Wide-open mouths.

Then while we were *sinking* our honest teeth into new victuals—all the humors of the street gathered together and crowded around to try and spoil our dinner.

And this is the way *matters* stand for us at the moment. We can hear the bold barking of the lap dogs: Izmailov, Filosofov, Yasinsky, and the rest of the ringtails.

Proof, by the way, that man wants to be a quadruped: That's what you get when you put Merezhkovsky together with Filosofov, Balmont with Gorodetsky, Briusov with Ellis.

Now hear this: the future casts its shadow over language.

The essence of Briu-Bal-Merezh: they begged for mercy from the expected conqueror, they had visions of disaster from the East, and in advance they begged the bent-browed Samurai, "Spare my Life! Oh, have mercy on me among the poor flies of this world!"

Libra is a forward-looking, expedient surrender. Every line in it is a *vicious* lie, afraid of strength and righteous anger the way others are afraid of vicious lies. All the strong, robust words in the Russian language have been banished from the pages of *Libra*. Their *Libra* is a little lapdog, doing its tricks and waving its paws at the West, yelping to proclaim its complete innocence in front of the yellow wolfhound.

But every line we write breathes victory and challenge, the bad temper of a conqueror, underground explosions, howls. We are a volcano. We vomit forth black smoke.

The heavens open and out comes an imposing
Pile of garbage; it looks a lot like Leo Tolstoy.

Remember that, you people!

Pushkin is an effete tumbleweed, blown hither and thither and even yon by the winds of indulgence.

Tolstoy's first teacher was that ox who wouldn't resist the butcher, but followed him stupidly to the slaughter house.

But our burning eyes see Victory ahead, and we have broken ranks to forge knife blades to replace the flint arrowheads of the year 1914. In 1914 we had to take cover—in 1915 we take over!

Remember the bull of Aragon!

In 1914 we lured out into the arena a bull with a beautiful coat, in 1915 his knees began to buckle and he fell over right in the arena. And from the quivering bull mouth flows a river of saliva (praising the victor).

Meanwhile our own development proceeds along artistic lines, Byron's, for instance (we always use our elders as a model).

Screams of anger from the jurors—from the fifty-kopeck-a-line men, the journalistic hawkers and hackmen (there's some justification; after all, they've all got families, and they can never catch up with the shadow of our moving locomotive). A hundred thousand of them from asylums and shelters, from maternity wards, all eating at our expense, and they eat better than usual. The doctors and lawyers hurl their angry thunderbolts.

And still we continue to grow.

We were not joking when we announce ourselves "He Who Appears," since in plain fact (1) we (2) have appeared.

All the Izmailovs and Yaskinskys have spilt the milk of their displeasure. Welcome this race of milch cows, they're a better breed than the Holmogorsky. Who are the milch cows? Izmailov, Filosofov, Yasinsky, and the rest, the hawkers and hackmen who "tickle" the readers' armpits. Bye-bye bulls.

The bullfighter waves his hat and disappears.

We have made it very clear that 20th century man is dragging around a thousand-year-old corpse (the past), doubled over like an ant trying to move a log. We alone have given man back his own true stature, and tossed away the truss of the past (the Tolstoys, the Homers, the Pushkins).

For those who have died but are still wandering about, we have exclamation marks made of ashwood.

For us, all freedoms have combined to form one fundamental freedom: freedom from the dead, i.e., from all these gentlemen who have lived before us.

The realm of numbers has the signs ∞ and 0: everything and nothing. For our enemies everything from Germany eastward was nothing, everything westward = ∞, everything. They never lived, they only drooled with envy at those who did live—over there. We have put these signs where they really belong, and taught the ruling class (M. et Mme. Corpse) how to live.

Above the dark precipice of our ancestors, beneath looming masses of rock, the entire country picks its way on goat feet down the steep cliff face of the present; it steps sure-footedly on ledges in the wall—allusions we have majestically let fall, our three-line Korans (for instance "Incantation by Laughter" and "We want to say 'hi' to the stars"), skipping from one foothold in the wall to the next, occasionally stopping to rest, elegant as a mountain goat. Eagles watch over its progress.

The Trumpet of the Martians

People of Earth, hear this!

The human brain until now has been hopping around on three legs (the three axes of location)! We intend to refurrow the human brain and to give this puppy dog a fourth leg—namely, the axis of TIME.

Poor lame puppy! Your obscene barking will no longer grate on our ears!

People from the past were no smarter than us; they thought the sails of government could be constructed only for the axes of space.

But now we appear, wrapped in a cloak of nothing but victories, and begin to build a union of youth with its sail tied to the axis of TIME, and we warn you in advance that we work on a scale bigger than Cheops, and our task is bold, majestic, and uncompromising.

We are uncompromising carpenters, and once again we throw ourselves and our names into the boiling kettles of unprecedented projects.

We believe in ourselves, we reject with indignation the vicious whispers of people from the past who still delude themselves that they can bite at our heels. Are we not gods? And are we not unprecedented in this: *our steadfast betrayal of our own past,* just as it barely reaches the age of victory, and our steadfast rage, raised above the planet like a hammer whose time has come? Planet Earth begins to shake already at the heavy tread of our feet!

Boom, you black sails of time!

Victor Khlebnikov, Maria Siniakova,
Bozhidar, Grigory Petnikov,
Nikolai Aseev

"LET THE MILKY WAY BE SPLIT INTO THE MILKY WAY OF INVENTOR/EXPLORERS AND THE MILKY WAY OF INVESTOR/ EXPLOITERS"

Here is the slogan for a new holy war.

Our questions are shouted into outer space, where human beings have never yet set foot.

We will brand them in powerful letters on the forehead of the Milky Way, stamp them upon the circular divinity of businessmen—questions like how to free our winged engine from its fat caterpillar, the freight train of previous generations. *Let age groups separate and live apart!* We have broken open the freight cars attached to the locomotive of our daring—and they contain nothing but tombstones for the young.

There are seven of us. We want a sword forged from the purest steel of youth. Those who have drowned in the laws of the family and the laws of trade, those who know only the expression "I consume," they will not understand us, since none of those things concerns us.

The right to form worldwide organizations according to age groups. Complete separation of age groups, the right to a separate way of life and separate activities. The right to have everything separate right up to and including the Milky Way. And out of the way with the uproar of age groups! Long rule the resonant sound of discontinuous time periods, white and black tablets and the brush of destiny. All who are closer to death than to birth must surrender! They must bite the dust when we attack like wild men in this time-war. But *we* have studied the soil of the continent of time, and we found it fruitful. But unrelenting hands from *back there* grabbed us, and they keep us from carrying out our beautiful betrayal of space. Has there ever been anything more intoxicating than this betrayal? You! What better answer is there to the danger of being born a man than to *carry off time?* We summon you toward a land where the trees speak, a land where there are scholarly unions as regular as waves, a land of springtime armies of love, *where time blossoms like the locust tree* and moves like a piston, where a superman in a carpenter's apron saws time into boards and like a turner of wood can shape his own tomorrow. (Oh, equations of kisses—You! Oh death ray, killed by the death ray in the trough of the wave.) We young people were moving toward that land, and all of a sudden some bony figure, someone dead, grabs us and tries to keep us from losing the feathers of the idiot TODAY. Is that fair?

Raise high the winged sails of time, you government of young people, now comes the second time we raid the flame of the investor/exploiters. Be bold! Push yesterday back, take away its bony hands, let the attack of a Balashov gouge out those horrible eyes. This is another sock in the eye for the vulgar inhabitants of space. Which is greater: S/T or N/R? The investor/exploiters in snarling packs have always slunk behind the inventor/explorers, now the inventor/explorers drive the investor/exploiters away.

Every industry of present-day Planet Earth—from the point of view and in the language and style of the investor/exploiters themselves—is "a steal" from the first inventor/explorer: Gauss. He founded the study of lightning. Yet while he was alive he didn't even get 150 rubles a year from his scientific work. Your memorials and laudatory articles try to justify the glee you feel at stealing him totally blind. And to pacify the rumblings of your conscience (which is suspiciously located in your vermiform appendix). Your supposed idols—Pushkin and Lermontov—met their deaths at your hands, in a field at the edge of town like rabid dogs! *You* sent Lobachevsky to be a parochial schoolteacher. Montgolfier wound up in a madhouse. And what about us? The militant vanguard of the inventor/explorers?

Here are your triumphs! Enough of them to fill several big books!

That is why the inventor/explorers, in full consciousness of their particular nature, their different way of life and their special mission, separate themselves from the investor/exploiters in order to form an independent government of *time* (no longer dependent on space), and put up a line of iron bars between ourselves and *them*. The future will decide who winds up in the zoo, inventor/explorers or investor/exploiters, who winds up chomping at the iron bars.

V. Khlebnikov

ORDERS

I. All the illustrious participants in Futurian publications are hereby promoted from the ranks of human beings to the ranks of Martians.

Signed: Velimir I, King of Time

II. The following are invited to become honorary nonvoting members of the Martian Council: H. G. Wells and Marinetti.

SUBJECTS FOR DISCUSSION

"Alloo, Alloo, Martians!"

1. How can we free ourselves from being dominated by people from the past who still retain a shadow of power in the world of space, without soiling ourselves by coming into contact with their lives (we can use the soap of word-creation), and leave them to drown in the destiny they have earned for themselves, that of malicious termites? We are fated to fight with *rhythm and time* for our right to be free from the filthy habits of people from past centuries, and to win that right.

2. How can we free the speeding locomotive of the younger generation from the insolent freight train of the older generation, hitched on without our permission?

Old ones! You are holding back the fast advance of humanity, you are preventing the boiling locomotive of youth from crossing the mountain that lies in *its* path. We have broken the locks and see what your freight cars contain: tombstones for the young.

You've hooked your earthling wagon to our star, our locomotive and its defiant whistle, hoping for a free ride!

[1916]

An Appeal by the Presidents of Planet Earth

We alone are the Government of Planet Earth. Which comes as no surprise. There's no doubt about it. We are uncontestable and recognized by everyone.

We have rolled up your three years of war into a single conch shell, a terrifying trumpet, and now we sing and shout and we roar out the terrible truth: the Government of Planet Earth already exists. We are it.

We alone, standing on the rock of ourselves and our names, with the ocean of your evil eyes beating all around us, have dared to call ourselves the Government of Planet Earth. We are it.

What insolence, people will say, but we will smile upon them like gods.

We hereby state that we do not recognize any overlords who call themselves governments, states, fatherlands, and other such business establishments and publishing houses, who have built the mercenary mills of their well-being beside the three-year-long waterfall of your beer and our blood, the streams made in 1917 of blood-red waves.

You cover the eyes of War with a homespun blind of words about the death penalty, mouthing the word "homeland" and setting up front-line court-martials.

Ahhl–aboard! Who will be our friend and comrade on this great journey?

We praise the trainloads of loyal subjects of her Holiness Spring and her people, who cling like swarms of bees to trains about to collapse beneath the weight of their new passenger—*Peace*. We know it is Spring who calls her people and sees them and smiles a sad smile.

So say we, ambassadors and commissars of Planet Earth.

And you governments of space, calm down, fix the kerchiefs on your heads and stop wailing as if you were attending your own funerals; nobody's going to hurt you. You will be able to enjoy the protection of our laws, you will become simply private associations, on an equal footing with anti-gopher societies, Dante societies, groups in favor of railroad sidings, or societies for the dissemination of information on the latest advances in threshing machines.

We promise not to lay a finger on you.

Our difficult assignment is to be switchmen on the tracks that join the Past and the Future.

You simply stay as you are—voluntary agreements between private persons, totally unnecessary, unimportant, boring, and dull as a toothache in the mouth of an old lady in the 17th century.

If you are so moral, you governments, then why these sacrifices for the gods, why are we crushed in your jaws, we soldiers and workers?

And if you are evil, then who among us will raise a finger to prevent your destruction?

We are endowed with reason, and we contemplate death with the same equanimity as a farmer who contemplates replacing one plow with a better one. Your space government of sinister plunder, you Kings and Kaisers and Sultans, is as different from our society as the hand of an ape burned by its unknown fire-god is different from the hand of a rider calmly holding the reins of bridled fate.

And that's not all. We are founding a society for the protection of governments of space from savage attack by the young rulers of Planet Earth. And this new class will crop your ears.

They are young and impolite—forgive any gaps in their upbringing. We are a special type of weapon. Comrade workers, do not complain because we follow a special path toward our common goal. Each type of weapon has its own design and its own laws. We are architect-workers.

Let these words be a gauntlet whose time has come:

THE GOVERNMENT OF PLANET EARTH

Whose black banner of unrule was raised by the hand of man and has been already snatched up by the hand of the universe. Who will tear down these black suns? The burning colors of these black suns? The enemy?

By right of preeminence and by assertion of our right of seizure, WE are the Government of Planet Earth. We and nobody else.

signed: V. Khlebnikov
G. Petnikov

We hope that this list will soon bear the brilliant names of Mayakovsky, Burliuk, and Gorky.

An I.D. for the government of stars.

[1917]

Ourselves and Our Buildings. Creators of Streetsteads

Proclamor!

Swaying beneath the weight of our armor, we poke mankind with the toe of our boot, sit back in the saddle, and point out the way! Then we ram his tired flanks with the little iron wheel attached to our boot, and the tired animal gathers for the jump and takes it idly, waving his tail with satisfaction.

We ride high in the saddle and shout: that's the way we want to go, toward those glass sunflowers in the iron shrubbery, toward cities whose patterns are as harmonious as a fisherman's net stretched out on the beach, cities of glass, shiny as inkwells, who compete among themselves for sunshine and a scrap of sky as if they were part of the vegetable kingdom. "Sunward" is written upon them in the terrifying alphabet of iron consonants and vowels of glass!

And if people are the salt of the earth, shouldn't we pass the saltcellar (the salt-solar!) sunward? We lay our massive hand upon the contemporary city and its planners and we shout: "Get rid of these rats' nests," and the terrifying rush of our breathing changes the air. We Futurians observe with pleasure that many things shatter beneath our mailed fist. The tables of victors are already hurled down, and the victors are already drinking our Mares' Milk, the drink of the steppe; a quiet moan comes from the vanquished.

We will now tell you about your city, and about ours.

I

Characteristics of the supposedly beautiful cities of the bygoners (ancestral architecture).

1. The bird's-eye view: at present, from directly overhead,

cities look like currycombs, like hairbrushes. Will it be like that in a city of winged inhabitants? In actual fact, the hand of time will turn the axis of vision upright, carrying away with it even that piece of architectural pomposity, the right angle. People now look at a city from the side; in the future they will look from directly overhead. The roof will become the main thing, the axis of the standing structure. With swarms of flyers and the face of the street above it, the city will begin to be concerned about its roofs and not its walls. Consider the roof as a thing in itself. It basks in the blue, far from dirty clouds of dust. A roof has no desire to imitate a pavement, to sweep itself clean with a broom composed of lungs, windpipes, and teary eyes; it will not sweep up its dust with eyelashes, or use lungs to sponge the black dirt off its body. Dress up your roofs! Think of them as hairdos, add some pretty pins. People will no longer gather in the vicious streets, whose dirty desire reduces human beings to residue in a washbasin; rather they will throng upon rooftops, beautiful young rooftops, waving their handkerchiefs after a giant levitating air-cloud, sending goodbyes and farewells after their departing friends.

How are they dressed? In suits of armor made from black or white linen, greaves, breastplates, gauntlets, gorgets, all stiffened and ironed, so that they always go around in armor the color of snow or of soot, cold, hard, even though they get soaked through in the first rainfall. Suits of linen armor. Instead of plumes fastened to their helmets, some of them wear smoking pitch. Some of them exchange bold, refined glances of condescension. Which is why the walkway runs higher than the windows and gutters and downspouts. People throng the rooftops, while the ground is left for the transport of goods; the city becomes a network of intersecting bridges, whose inhabited arches connect the residential towers that serve as their supports; the residential buildings serve the bridge as piers and as walls for shaft areas. The city crowds will no longer move about on foot or on their four-legged colleagues; they will have learned to fly above the city, raining their glances upon the place below; above the city will hover a cloud that will test its builder's work, a threat to weak roofs, like a thunderstorm or tornado. People on the rooftops will wrest from any groundling unreserved praise to the roof, and to the street that passes above the buildings. And so, behold its contours! A street high above the city, and the eye of the crowd high above the street!

2. The city seen from the side: the so-called "beautiful" cities of the present day, seen from a certain distance, look like junkpiles. They have forgotten the rule of alternation that older structures (Greek, Islam) knew, alternation of the density of stone with the immateriality of air (Voronikhin's cathedral), the alternation of substance and void; a similar relationship between stressed and unstressed syllable is the essence of a line of verse. City streets today have no perceptible pulse. It is as hard to look at streets all lumped together as it is to read words without spaces between them, or to speak words without stress or accent. What we need is a street with variation, where the heights of the buildings are the accent marks, so to speak, providing a variation in the breathing of the stone. Present-day buildings are built according to the well-known rule for cannons: find a mold and fill it with molten metal. It's the same thing: take a blueprint and fill it up with stone. But in a blueprint there is something that exists and is ponderable, namely the line, which is absent from the building, and contrariwise: the ponderability of a building's walls is absent from the blueprint, which seems empty; so that the reality of the blueprint corresponds to the nonreality of the building, and vice versa. The designers take the blueprint and fill it with stone, i.e., over the course of centuries, without even noticing, they have multiplied the fundamental ratio of stone and void by minus one, which is why the most grotesque buildings may have the most elegant blueprints, and a Scriabin of a blueprint can produce a junkbin of a building. It is time to put a stop to this! Blueprints are only good for constructing buildings of wire, since the idea of replacing a line with a void and the void with stone is the same as calling the Holy Father—*il Papa*—the friend of *Mama Roma*. The outer surfaces are ruined by a muddle of windows, by the detailing of drainpipes, petty stupidities of design, nonsensicalities, which is why the majority of buildings still in scaffoldings are better than when they are finished. The contemporary tenement apartment building (the art of the bygoners) is an outgrowth of the medieval castle; but castles were freestanding buildings surrounded by air, self-

sufficient as hermits, resembling a loud interjection! in the landscape. But here, flattened out by their contiguous walls, depriving one another of decent views, squeezed into the spawn of the streets—what have they come to resemble, with their jumpy patterns of windows, but lines in a book you try to read on a train! Isn't this the way flowers die, clutched too tightly in a clumsy hand, just like these rats'-nest buildings? These descendants of castles?

3. What serves to ornament cities? On the threshold of its beauty stand factory chimneys. The three smoking chimneys on the south embankment of the Moscow River call to mind a candlestick and three candles invisible in daylight. But the forest of chimneys on the lifeless northern swamp forces us to witness nature shifting from one order to another; this is the soft, tender moss of a second-order forest; the city itself becomes a first experiment in a higher-order growth, as yet amateurish. Those swamps are a clearing of silky chimney moss. The chimneys are golden-haired delights.

4. Inside the city. Very few people have realized that to entrust the development of streets to the greed and stupidity of landlords and to give them the right to build buildings is to reduce life to nothing more than unwarranted solitary confinement; the gloomy life that goes on inside a tenement building is hardly distinguishable from solitary confinement; it resembles the life of an oarsman confined beneath the deck of a galley: he waves an oar in the air once a month, and the monster greed of a dark and alien will proceeds toward its dubious goals.

5. Few have realized as well that traveling is unpleasant and totally devoid of comfort.

II

Remedies from the yet-to-be city of the Futurians:

1. The idea is this: a container of molded glass, a mobile dwelling module supplied with a door, with attachment couplings, mounted on wheels, with its inhabitant inside it. It is set on a train (special gauge, with racks specially designed to hold such modules), or a steamship, and inside, without ever leaving

it, its inhabitant would travel to his destination. Expandable on occasion, the glass cubicle is suitable for spending the night. Once it was decided that the primary building unit would be no longer an incidental material like brick, but rather these modular units inhabited by individuals, they began the construction of framework-buildings whose open spaces were filled in by the inhabitants themselves with their moveable glass cubicles. And these units were able to be transported from one building to another. Thus was a great achievement attained: it was no longer the single individual who traveled, but his house on wheels or, more precisely, his booth, capable of being attached to a flatrack on a train or to a steamship.

Just as a tree in winter lives in anticipation of leaves or needles, so these framework-buildings, these grillworks full of empty spaces, spread their arms like steel junipers and awaited their glass occupants. They looked like unloaded, unarmed vessels, or like the gallows tree, or like a desolate city in the mountains. And they gave everyone the right to own such a habitation in any city. Every city in the land, wherever a proprietor may decide to move in his glass cubicle, was required to offer a location in one of these framework-buildings for the mobile dwelling-module (the glass hut). And with a whine of chains the traveler in his glass cocoon is hoisted aloft.

For the sake of this innovation, the form and dimensions of all dwelling units will be identical throughout the entire country. There will be a number on the glass surface to indicate the proprietor's place in the arrangement. He himself will be able to sit quietly reading as they move him into space. And in this way, we create proprietors: (1) not on the basis of land ownership, but only on the right to a space in a framework-building; (2) not in any one particular city, but generally in any city in the country that takes part in this union for citizen exchange. And all this in order to serve the needs of a mobile population.

Whole cities consisted of such frameworks, products of the joint labor of glassmakers and Ural steelworkers. Every city would have such a half-occupied iron framework waiting for glass occupants, like a skeleton without muscles, the cells for the insertable glass cubicles, which are like a currency of volume, appearing empty and dark. And everywhere boats and trains on the move, laden with these glass cubicles, moving them from place to place. Similar framework-hotels were constructed at the beaches, beside lakes, near mountains and rivers. Sometimes one owner would have two or three such cages. (1) Sleeping rooms in the buildings would alternate with living rooms, dining rooms, cookerys. (2) Contemporary rats'-nest buildings are built through a combination of stupidity and greed. Whereas their predecessors, the freestanding castles of the Middle Ages, extended their power over the area around them, these sardine-castles squeezed sideways next to one another along the street exert their power inward, over the people who live inside them. In the unequal struggle between the many who inhabit a building and the one who owns it, the many, innocent of any blood-letting, nevertheless live in confinement, in the dark prison of these tenements, oppressed by the heavy hand of this combination of stupidity and greed; the only relief available to them has come first from private associations, then from the government. It has been recognized that the city is a focal point for rays of social force, and is thus in certain measure the property of all the inhabitants of the country, and that in his attempt to live in a city a citizen of the country cannot simply be thrown (by one of those who has just happened to take the city away from him) into the stone huddle of a rats' nest, there to live the life of a prisoner, especially one condemned not by the court system but by the mere facts of existence. But what difference does it make to the prisoner? Even if he doesn't suspect the dreadful uniformity of the living quarters around him, he has been harshly condemned, whether by existence or by the court system; he has been cast into a dark hole like a prisoner of war and cut off from the rest of the world.

It had become clear that the construction of dwellings was legitimately the business of those who would have to live in them. The first beginnings were made when individual streets joined together to form a shareholders' association, in order to construct communal habitats, streetsteads, whose design was based on the principle of alternation of mass and void, thus exchanging the street as a filthy container for a street conceived as a single beautiful habitat; this arrangement was based on the system used in old Novgorod. Here is a view of the great Tver street: a tall townstead built of logs surrounded by an open square. A slender tower connected by a bridge to the neighboring streetstead. Wall-buildings stand next to each other, like three books standing on end.

A residential tower is connected by two suspension bridges to another tall, slender tower just like it, and yet another courtstead. It all resembles a garden. The buildings are connected by bridges, the elevated walkways of the townstead. Thus were the idiosyncratic horrors of private architecture avoided. An organic poison began to take effect, combatting the arsenic of earlier architecture. Private enterprise still possessed the right to build buildings (1) outside the cities, (2) on the outskirts, (3) in rural areas and wasteland, but even so only for personal use. At a later period governmental authority became involved in streetstead-planning, and the concept of the public habitat came into being.

By assuming the authority for urban planning and defining its concern for the problem of houslings and houseability, the government became the senior builder in the land. Standing upon the debris of private architecture, it rested upon the shield of gratitude of those who had suffered torments in the rats' nests of the present day.

They realized that it was ethical to take a profit from the building of glass dwellings. All those who had suffered from the indifferent attitude "sink or swim" were taken under the wing of the architect-government.

The decree against private architecture was never extended to rural dwellings, peasant huts, family dwellings, or farmsteads. The war was being waged only against the urban rats' nests. Land occupied by farmsteaders remained in the hands of its previous owners. The urban habitats were: (1) leased out to societies set up by the cities, groups of physicians, travel societies, street associations, parishes; (2) remained with the builder; (3) were sold upon conditions that controlled greed and restricted landlords' rights. This provided an enormous source of revenues. The tall glass towers of the townstead, constructed along the coast and in picturesque locations, became part of the beauty of the locale. And so the government became the chief builder of the nation, and this happened because its resources made it the most powerful of all private societies.

3. What kinds of structures were built? (A word of warning here. We are going to speak now about the marvelous monsters of the Futurian imagination, which will have replaced the public squares of the present day, dirty as the soul of Izmailov.)

(a) Bridge-buildings: structures where the arches of a bridge and its support pilings are both composed of dwelling units. Some of these glass and steel honeycombs served as part of an access bridge to neighboring structures. This was known as a bridgestead. Support towers and a hemispherical arch. Bridgesteads were often built over a river.

(b) The poplar-tree-building consisted of a narrow tower sheathed from top to bottom by rings of glass cubicles. There was an elevator in the tower, and each sun-space had its own private access to the interior shaft, which resembled an enormous bell tower (700–1400 feet high). The top of the building served as a landing platform. The rings of sun-spaces were closely packed together to a very great height. The glass sheath and its dark frame gave the building its resemblance to a poplar tree.

(c) Underwater palaces: for auritoriums. These were underwater palaces built of thick glass blocks right down among the fishes, with views of the sea, and underwater hatches connecting them to dry land. There, in the silence of the deep, speech and rhetoric were taught.

(d) Steamship-buildings. An artificial reservoir constructed at a high elevation and filled with water, and a real steamship riding the waves, inhabited mainly by sailors.

(e) The filament-building consisted of single rooms connected in a single strand stretched between two towers. Dimensions 20 × 700 × 700 feet. Lots of light! But not much room. A thousand inhabitants. Quite suitable for hotels, hospitals, for construction upon mountaintops or at the coast. Transparent because of the glass sun-spaces, it had the appearance of a filament or film. Very attractive at night, when it resembled a thread of fire strung between the dark gloomy needle-towers. Built on hilltops. An excellent example of the possibilities of the framework-building.

(f) A similar building with a second strand of rooms.

(g) The checkerboard-building. Where empty room-slots were arranged to form a checkerboard pattern.

(h) The swing-building. A chain fixed between two factory chimneys, with a little dwelling-house hung on it. Suitable for thinkers, sailors, or Futurians.

(i) The strand-of-hair-building consists of a lateral axis with strands of Futurian rooms ascending next to it, to a height of 700–1400 feet. Sometimes as many as three of these strands twine along a steel needle.

(j) The goblet building; a steel stalk 350–1400 feet high supporting a glass dome containing four or five rooms. Private apartments for those who had retired from the earth; set upon a base of steel beams.

(k) The tube-building consisted of a double sheet of rooms curved to form a tube enclosing a spacious courtyard containing a waterfall.

(l) In the form of an open book; this one consists of stone walls set at an angle, and glass sheets of living modules arranged fanwise between these walls. This is the book-building. The walls are 700–1400 feet high.

(m) The field-building, in which great floors serve to support a tranquil, deserted space, free of interior walls, upon which in artistic disarray are scattered glass huts, lean-tos that don't reach the ceiling, self-contained wigwams and tepees; deer antlers, those rough-hewn products of nature, hung upon the walls and gave each circle the look of a hunter's shack. The corners contained places to bathe privately. Often these floors rose one over the other in the form of a pyramid.

(n) The house on wheels. On a long oil-eater with one or more dwelling modules; living quarters, a secular travelstead for 20th century gypsies.

Principles:

1. Fixed framework-buildings, mobile dwelling-modules.

2. Individuals travel by train without ever leaving the living space.

3. The right to private possession of a living space in any city.

4. Construction carried out by the public sector.

5. Regulation for the construction of private houses; an end to streets (as they presently exist); the rhythmic design of habitats, towers as points of interjection in the landscape.

A journey described. I sat in my dwelling-module reading an elegant poem composed of the four words *go-um, mo-um, su-um,* and *tu-um;* I pondered its meaning, which seemed to me more beautiful than many longer poems designed only to destroy euphony. Without leaving I was carried by train across the continent to the seacoast, where I intended to visit my sister. I was aware of scraping noises, of a gentle rocking. That was the steel chain that hoisted me into a poplar-tree-building. Dwelling units in the glass sheath and occasional faces flickered past. A sudden stop. Here in one of the building's empty cells I left my living space. Dressed in the building's style of dress, I stopped at the waterfall and walked out onto one of the small bridges. Elegant, slender, it joined two poplar-tree-buildings at a height of 600 feet. I bowed my head and began to recompute myself, to learn what I had to do in order to comply with its power within me. In the distance a filament-building hung between its two steel needles: a thousand glass living units glittered in the air, like a string of trailers suspended between two towers. This was a residence for artists; they enjoyed a double view of the ocean, since the building and its two towers rose near the water. It looked very beautiful in the evening. Beside it a flower-building rose gracefully to an unattainable height; it had a dome of reddish matte glass, lacy railings that formed the edge of the calyx, and staircases of beautifully wrought steel. This was the house where I and E lived. The steel needles of the filament-building and a dense fabric of glass honeycombs glowed in the sunset. From the corner tower, another building stretched away in a lateral direction. Two strand-buildings stretched upwards twining around each other. Before me stood a checkerboard-building. I was full of thought. A grove of glassy poplar-tree-buildings lined the shore. Meanwhile four "Chaika 11's" carried an airborne net with bathers sitting on it, and set them down next to the water. It was time for a swim. They rocked side by side upon the water. I thought about fairy-tale flying horses, about magic carpets; what *were* fairy tales really, I wondered: merely an old man's memory? Or were they visions of a future only children can foresee? I thought, in other words, about the flood and the destruction of Atlantis: had it already happened, or was it yet in the future? I was rather inclined to think it was yet in the future.

I stood on the bridge; I was full of thought.

The Head of the Universe. Time in Space

Two theses:

1. There are ways of looking at a new form of creativity, the art of number blocks, where a number artist can freely draw the inspired head of the universe as he sees it turned toward him. He is not a child; he has no need of the cages and boundaries of the separate scientific disciplines. Proclaiming a free triangle with three points—the world, the artist, and the number—he draws the ear or the mouth of the universe with the broad brush of numbers. He executes his strokes freely in scientific space, and he knows that number serves the human mind in the same way that charcoal serves the artist's hand, or clay and chalk the hand of the sculptor. Working with number as his charcoal, he unites all previous human knowledge in his art. A single one of his lines provides an immediate lightninglike connection between a red corpuscle and Earth, a second precipitates into helium, a third shatters upon the unbending heavens and discovers the satellites of Jupiter. Velocity is infused with a new speed, the speed of thought, while the boundaries that separate different areas of knowledge will disappear before the procession of liberated numbers cast into print like orders throughout the whole of Planet Earth.

Here they are then, these ways of looking at the new form of creativity, which we think is perfectly workable.

The surface of Planet Earth is 510,051,300 square kilometers; the surface of a red corpuscle—that citizen and star of man's Milky Way—0.000,128 square millimeters. These citizens of the sky and the body have concluded a treaty, whose provision is this: the surface of the star Earth divided by the surface of the tiny corpuscular star equals 365 times 10 to the tenth power (365×10^{10}). A beautiful concordance of two worlds, one that establishes man's right to first place on the Earth. This is the first article of the treaty between the government of blood cells and the government of heavenly bodies. A living walking Milky Way and his tiny star have concluded a 365-point agreement with the Milky Way in the sky and its great earth star. The dead Milky Way and the living one have affixed their signatures to it as two equal and legal entities.

2. In several of Malevich's shaded-in sketches, his encrustations of black planes and spheres, I have found that the ratio of the largest shaded area to the smallest black circle is 365. These collections of planes therefore contain a shade-year and a shade-day. Once more in the realm of painting I had observed time commanding space. In the consciousness of this artist, white and black are sometimes engaged in a real conflict and sometimes vanish completely, yielding place to pure dimension.

[1919]

To the Artists of the World

A Written Language for Planet Earth: A Common System of Hieroglyphs for the People of Our Planet

We have long been searching for a program that would act something like a lens, capable of focusing the combined rays of the work of the artist and the work of the thinker toward a single point where they might join in a common task and be able to ignite even the cold essence of ice and turn it to a blazing bonfire. Such a program, the lens capable of directing together your fiery courage and the cold intellect of the thinker, has now been discovered.

The goal is to create a common written language shared by all the peoples of this third satellite of the Sun, to invent written symbols that can be understood and accepted by our entire star, populated as it is with human beings, and lost here in the universe. You can see that such a task is worthy of the time we live in. Painting has always used a language accessible to everyone. And the Chinese and Japanese peoples speak hundreds of different languages, but they read and write in one single written language. Languages have betrayed their glorious beginnings. There was once a time when words served to dispel enmity and make the future transparent and peaceful, and when languages, proceeding in stages, united the people of (1) a cave, (2) a settlement, (3) a tribe or kinship group, (4) a state, into a single rational world, a union of those who shared one single auditory instrument for the exchange of values and ideas. One savage caveman understood another and laid his blind weapon aside. Nowadays sounds have abandoned their past functions and serve the purposes of hostility; they have become differentiated auditory instruments for the exchange of rational wares; they have divided multilingual mankind into different camps involved in tariff wars, into a series of verbal marketplaces beyond whose confines any given language loses currency. Every system of auditory currency claims supremacy, and so languages as such serve to disunite mankind and wage spectral wars. Let us hope that one single written language may henceforth accompany the long-term destinies of mankind and prove to be the new vortex that unites us, the new integrator of the human race. Mute graphic marks will reconcile the cacophony of languages.

To the artists who work with ideas falls the task of creating an alphabet of concepts, a system of basic units of thought from which words may be constructed.

The task of artists who work with paint is to provide graphic symbols for the basic units of our mental processes.

We have now accomplished that part of that labor which was the thinkers' task; we stand now on the first landing of the staircase of thinkers, and we find there the artists of China and Japan, who were already ahead of us, and our greetings to them! Here is what we see from our place on that staircase: the vista of a shared human alphabet that our place on the staircase of thinkers reveals. For the moment, without advancing any proof, I maintain:

1. B (*v*) in all languages means the turning of one point around another, either in a full circle or only a part of one, along an arc, up or down.
2. X (*kh*) means a closed curve that shields the location of one point from the movement toward it of another point (a protective line).
3. З (*z*) means the reflection of a moving point from the surface of a mirror at an angle equal to the angle of incidence. The impact of a ray upon a solid surface.
4. M (*m*) means the disintegration of a certain quantity into infinitely small parts (within certain limits) equal as a whole to the original quantity.
5. Ш (*sh*) means the merging of several surfaces into a single surface and the merging of the boundaries between them. The striving of the one-dimensional world of any given dimension to describe a larger area of a two-dimensional world.
6. П (*p*) means the increase along a straight line of the empty space between two points, the movement along a straight line of one point away from another and, as

in the sum of a point set, the rapid growth in the volume occupied by a certain number of points.

7. Ч (*ch*) means the empty space of one body containing the volume of another body, in such a way that the negative volume of the first body is exactly equal to the positive volume of the second. This is a hollow two-dimensional world that serves as an envelope for a three-dimensional body—within certain limits.
8. Л (*l*) means the diffusion of the smallest possible waves on the widest possible surface perpendicular to a moving point, the height vanishing with the increase in width, for a given volume the height becomes infinitely small as the other two axes become infinitely large. The formation of a two-dimensional body out of a three-dimensional one.
9. К (*k*) means the absence of motion, a set of *n* points at rest, the preservation of their relative positions; the termination of movement.
10. С (*s*) means a fixed point that serves as a point of departure for the motion of many other points which begin their trajectory there.
11. Т (*t*) means a direction, wherein a fixed point creates an absence of motion among a set of motions in the same direction, a negative trajectory and its direction beyond a fixed point.
12. Д (*d*) means the transposition of a point from one system of points to another system, which is then transformed by the addition of that point.
13. Г (*g*) means the largest possible oscillations, whose height is perpendicular to the motion and which are extended along the axis of motion. Movements of maximum height.
14. Н (*n*) means the absence of points, an empty field.
15. Б (*b*) means the meeting of two points moving along a straight line from opposite directions. Their clash, the reversal of one point by the impact of the other.
16. Ц (*ts*) means the passage of one body through an empty space in another.

17. Щ (*shch*) means the laying out of a whole surface into separate sections, the volume remaining fixed.
18. Р (*r*) means the division of a smooth hollow body as a trace of the movement of another body through it.
19. Ж (*zh*) means motion out of a closed volume, the separation of free point systems.

So then, from our landing on the staircase of thinkers, it has become clear that the simple bodies of a language—the sounds of the alphabet—are the names of various aspects of space, an enumeration of the events of its life. The alphabet common to a multitude of peoples is in fact a short dictionary of the spatial world that is of such concern to your art, painters, and to your brushes.

Each individual word resembles a small workers' collective, where the first sound of the word is like the chairman of the collective who directs the whole set of sounds in the word. If we assemble all the words that begin with the same consonantal sound, we observe that, just as meteors often fall from one single point in the sky, all these words fly from the single point of a certain conceptualization of space. And that point becomes the meaning of the sound of the alphabet, and its simplest name.

So for example the twenty names for buildings that begin with Х (*kh*), names of entities that protect the point of man from the hostile point of bad weather, cold or enemies, bear the burden of our second claim quite solidly on their shoulders.

The artists' task would be to provide a special sign for each type of space. Each sign must be simple and clearly distinguishable from all the rest. It might be possible to resort to the use of color, and to designate М (*m*) with dark blue, В (*v*) with green, Б (*b*) with red, С (*s*) with gray, Л (*l*) with white, and so on. But it might also be possible for this universal dictionary, the shortest in existence, to retain only graphic signs. Life, of course, will introduce its own corrections, but in life it has always been true that in the beginning the sign for a concept was a simple picture of that concept. And from that seed sprang up the tree of each individual letter's existence.

To me, В (*v*) appears in the form of a circle and a point within it. ⊙

Х (*kh*) in the form of a combination of two lines and a point. 

З (*z*) a kind of K fallen over on its back: a mirror and a ray. 

Л (*l*) a circular area and an axis line. 

Ч (*ch*) in the form of a goblet. 

С (*s*) a bundle of straight lines. 

But it is your task, you artists, to alter or improve these signs. If you succeed in constructing them, you will have put the finishing touches on the tasks that must be accomplished on this star we all share.

This proposed experiment to convert beyonsense language from an untamed condition to a domesticated one, to make it bear useful burdens, deserves a certain amount of attention.

After all, even in Sanskrit *vritti* means rotation, and in Egyptian as in Russian *khata* means hut.

A program for a single, universal, scientifically constructed language appears more and more clearly as a goal for humanity.

Your task, you artists, would be to construct a suitable instrument of exchange between auditory and visual modes, to construct a system of graphic signs that inspires confidence.

In the alphabet given above I have already provided a universal system of sound "images" for various aspects of space; now we must construct a second system, one of written signs, soundless currency for the marketplace of conversation.

I am confident you will avoid external influences and will follow your own creative paths.

I here offer the first experiments in beyonsense language as the language of the future (with one reservation, that vowels in what follows are incidental and serve the purposes of euphony):

Instead of saying:

> "The Hunnic and Gothic hordes, having united and gathered themselves about Attila, full of warlike enthusiasm, progressed further together, but having been met and defeated by Aetius, the protector of Rome, they scattered into numerous bands and settled and remained peacefully on

> their own lands, having poured out into and filled up the emptiness of the steppes."

Could we not say instead:

> "SHa + So (Hunnic and Gothic hordes), Ve Attila, CHa Po, So Do, but Bo + Zo Aetius, KHo of Rome, So Mo Ve + Ka So, Lo SHa of the steppes + CHa."

And that is what the first beyonsense story played upon the strings of the alphabet sounds like. Or:

> "Ve So of the human race Be Go of languages Pe of our minds Ve So SHa language, Bo Mo of words Mo Ka of thought CHa of sounds Po So Do Lu earth Mo So language, Ve earth."

Which is to say:

> "Intent upon uniting the human race, but meeting the barrier of the mountain chains of languages, the fire storm of our minds revolves around the idea of a communal beyonsense language and achieves the atomization of words into units of thought contained in an envelope of sounds and then rapidly and simultaneously proceeds toward the recognition throughout the earth of one single beyonsense language."

Of course, these attempts are nothing but a baby's first cry, and the labor all lies ahead of us, but the overall model of a universal language in the future is here provided. It will be "beyonsense."

[1919]

On Poetry

People say a poem must be understandable. Like a sign on the street, which carries the clear and simple words "For Sale." But a street sign is not exactly a poem. Though it is understandable. On the other hand, what about spells and incantations, what we call magic words, the sacred language of paganism, words like "shagadam, magadam, vigadam, pitz, patz, patzu"—they are rows of mere syllables that the intellect can make no sense of, and they form a kind of beyonsense language in folk speech. Nevertheless an enormous power over mankind is attributed to these incomprehensible words and magic spells, and direct influence upon the fate of man. They contain powerful magic. They claim the power of controlling good and evil and swaying the hearts of lovers. The prayers of many nations are written in a language incomprehensible to those who pray. Does a Hindu understand the Vedas? Russians do not understand Old Church Slavonic. Neither do Poles and Czechs understand Latin. But a prayer written in Latin works just as powerfully as the sign in the street. In the same way, the language of magic spells and incantations rejects judgments made by everyday common sense.

Its strange wisdom may be broken down into the truths contained in separate sounds: *sh, m, v,* etc. We do not yet understand these sounds. We confess that honestly. But there is no doubt that these sound sequences constitute a series of universal truths passing before the predawn of our soul. If we think of the soul as split between the government of intellect and a stormy population of feelings, then incantations and beyonsense language are appeals over the head of the government straight to the population of feelings, a direct cry to the predawn of the soul or a supreme example of the rule of the masses in the life of language and intellect, a lawful device reserved for rare occasions. Another example: Sophia Kovalevskaia owes her talent for mathematics, as she herself makes clear in her memoirs, to the fact that the walls of her nursery were covered with unusual wallpaper—pages of her uncle's book on advanced algebra. We must acknowledge that the world of mathematics is a restricted area as far as the feminine half of humanity is concerned. Kovalevskaia is one of the few mortals who has entered that world. Could a child of seven really have understood those symbols—equal signs, powers, brackets—all the magic marks of sums and subtractions? Of course not; nevertheless they exercised a decisive influence on her life, and it was under the influence of the childhood wallpaper that she became a famous mathematrix.

Similarly, the magic in a word remains magic even if it is not understood, and loses none of its power. Poems may be understandable or they may not, but they must be good, they must be real.

From the examples of the algebraic signs on the walls of Kovalevskaia's nursery that had such a decisive influence on the child's fate, and from the example of spells, it is clear that we cannot demand of all language: "be easy to understand, like the sign in the street." The speech of higher intelligence, even when it is not understandable, falls like seed into the fertile soil of the soul and only much later, in mysterious ways, does it bring forth its shoots. Does the earth understand the writing of the seeds a farmer scatters on its surface? No. But the grain still ripens in autumn, in response to those seeds. In any case, I certainly do not maintain that every incomprehensible piece of writing is beautiful. I mean only that we must not reject a piece of writing simply because it is incomprehensible to a particular group of readers. The claim has been made that poems about labor can be created only by people who work in factories. Is this true? Isn't the nature of a poem to be found in its withdrawal from itself, from its point of contact with everyday reality? Is a poem not a flight from the *I*? A poem is related to flight, in the shortest time possible its language must cover the greatest distance in images and thoughts.

. . . . .

. . . that there is no place to escape from the self. Inspiration always deludes itself about the poet's background. Medieval knights wrote about rustic shepherds, Lord Byron about pirates,

Buddha was a king's son who wrote in praise of poverty. Or the other way around: Shakespeare was convicted of theft but wrote in the language of kings, as did Goethe, the son of a modest burgher, and their writing is devoted to portrayals of court life. The tundras of the Pechersky region have never known warfare, yet there they preserve epic songs about Vladimir and his hero knights that have long since been forgotten in the Dnieper. If we consider artistic creativity as the greatest possible deviation of the string of thought from the axis of the creator's life, as a flight from the self, then we have good reason for believing that even poems about an assembly line will be written not by someone who works on an assembly line, but by someone from beyond the factory walls. It's always the other way around: once he withdraws from the assembly line, stretching the string of his soul to the fullest length, the assembly-line poet will either pass into the world of scientific imagery, of strange scientific visions, into the future of Planet Earth, like Gastev, or into the world of basic human values, like Alexandrovsky, into the subtle life of the heart.

The Radio of the Future

The Radio of the Future—the central tree of our consciousness—will inaugurate new ways to cope with our endless undertakings and will unite all mankind.

The main Radio station, that stronghold of steel, where clouds of wires cluster like strands of hair, will surely be protected by a sign with a skull and crossbones and the familiar word "Danger," since the least disruption of Radio operations would produce a mental blackout over the entire country, a temporary loss of consciousness.

Radio is becoming the spiritual sun of the country, a great wizard and sorcerer.

Let us try to imagine Radio's main station: in the air a spider's web of lines, a storm cloud of lightning bolts, some subsiding, some flaring up anew, crisscrossing the building from one end to the other. A bright blue ball of spherical lightning hanging in midair like a timid bird, guy wires stretched out at a slant.

From this point on Planet Earth, every day, like the flight of birds in springtime, a flock of news departs, news from the life of the spirit.

In this stream of lightning birds the spirit will prevail over force, good counsel over threats.

The activities of artists who work with the pen and brush, the discoveries of artists who work with ideas (Mechnikov, Einstein) will instantly transport mankind to unknown shores.

Advice on day-to-day matters will alternate with lectures by those who dwell upon the snowy heights of the human spirit. The crests of waves in the sea of human knowledge will roll across the entire country into each local Radio station, to be projected that very day as letters onto the dark pages of enormous books, higher than houses, that stand in the center of each town, slowly turning their own pages.

RADIO READING-WALLS

These books of the streets will be known as Radio Reading-Walls! Their giant dimensions frame the settlements and carry out the tasks of all mankind.

Radio has solved a problem that the church itself was unable to solve and has thus become as necessary to each settlement as a school is, or a library.

The problem of celebrating the communion of humanity's one soul, one daily spiritual wave that washes over the entire country every twenty-four hours, saturating it with a flood of scientific and artistic news—that problem has been solved by Radio using lightning as its tool. On the great illuminated books in each town Radio today has printed a story by a favorite writer, an essay on the fractional exponents of space, a description of airplane flights, and news about neighboring countries. Everyone can read whatever he chooses. This one book, identical across the entire country, stands in the center of every small town, always surrounded by a ring of readers, a carefully composed silent Reading-Wall in every settlement.

But now in black type, news of an enormous scientific discovery appears on the screens; a certain chemist, famous within the narrow circle of his followers, has discovered a method for producing meat and bread out of widely available types of clay.

A crowd gathers, wondering what will happen next.

Earthquakes, fires, disasters, the events of each twenty-four-hour period will be printed out on the Radio books. The whole country will be covered with Radio stations.

RADIOAUDITORIUMS

Surges of lightning are picked up and transmitted to the metal mouth of an auto-speaker, which converts them into amplified sound, into singing and human speech.

The entire settlement has gathered around to listen. The metal trumpet mouth loudly carries the news of the day, the activities of the government, weather information, events from the exciting life of the capital cities.

The effect will be like a giant of some kind reading a gigantic journal out loud. But it is only this metal town cryer, only the metal mouth of the auto-speaker; gravely and distinctly it announces the morning news, beamed to this settlement from the signal tower of the main Radio station.

But now what follows? Where has this great stream of sound come from, this inundation of the whole country in supernatural singing, in the sound of beating wings, this broad silver stream full of whistlings and clangor and marvelous mad bells surging from somewhere we are not, mingling with children's voices singing and the sound of wings?

Over the center of every town in the country these voices pour down, a silver shower of sound. Amazing silver bells mixed with whistlings surge down from above. Are these perhaps the voices of heaven, spirits flying low over the farmhouse roof? No . . . . .

The Mussorgsky of the future is giving a coast-to-coast concert of his work, using the Radio apparatus to create a vast concert hall stretching from Vladivostok to the Baltic, beneath the blue dome of the heavens.

On this one evening he bewitches the people, sharing with them the communion of his soul, and on the following day he is only an ordinary mortal again. The artist has cast a spell over his land; he has given his country the singing of the sea and the whistling of the wind. The poorest house in the smallest town is filled with divine whistlings and all the sweet delights of sound.

RADIO AND ART EXHIBITS

In a small town far away, a crowd of people gathers today in front of the great illuminated Radio screens, which rise up like giant books. Why? Because today Radio is using its apparatus to transmit images in color, to allow every little town in the entire country to take part in an exhibit of paintings being held in the capital city. This exhibit is transmitted by means of light impulses repeated in thousands of mirrors at every Radio station. If Radio previously acted as the universal ear, now it has become a pair of eyes that annihilate distance. The main Radio signal tower emits its rays, and from Moscow an exhibit of the best painters bursts into flower on the reading walls of every small town in this enormous country, on loan to every inhabited spot on the map.

RADIO CLUBS

Let's move up closer. Majestic skyscrapers wrapped in clouds, a game of chess between two people located at opposite ends of Planet Earth, an animated conversation between someone in America and someone in Europe. Now the reading-walls grow dark; suddenly the sound of a distant voice is heard singing, the metallic throat of Radio beams the rays of the song to its many metallic singers: metal sings! And its words, brought forth in silence and solitude, and their welling springs, become a communion shared by the entire country.

More obedient than strings beneath the violinist's hand, the metallic apparatus of Radio will talk and sing, obeying every marked pulse of the song.

Every settlement will have listening devices and metallic voices to serve one sense, metallic eyes to serve the other.

THE GREAT SORCERER

Finally we will have learned to transmit the sense of taste—and every simple, plain but healthful meal can be transformed by means of taste-dreams carried by Radio rays, creating the illusion of a totally different taste sensation.

People will drink water, and imagine it to be wine. A simple, ample meal will wear the guise of a luxurious feast. And thus will Radio acquire an even greater power over the minds of the nation.

In the future, even odors will obey the will of Radio: in the dead of winter the honey scent of linden trees will mingle with the odor of snow, a true gift of Radio to the nation.

Doctors today can treat patients long-distance, through hypnotic suggestion. Radio in the future will be able to act also as a doctor, healing patients without medicine.

And even more:

It is a known fact that certain notes like "la" and "ti" are able to increase muscular capacity, sometimes as much as sixty-four times, since they thicken the muscle for a certain length of time. During periods of intense hard work like summer harvest time, or during the construction of great buildings, these sounds can be broadcast by Radio over the entire country, increasing its collective strength enormously.

And, finally, the organization of popular education will pass into the hands of Radio. The Supreme Soviet of Sciences will broadcast lessons and lectures to all the schools of the country—higher institutions as well as lower.

The teacher will become merely a monitor while these lectures are in progress. The daily transmission of lessons and textbooks through the sky into the country schools of the nation, the unification of its consciousness into a single will.

Thus will Radio forge continuous links in the universal soul and mold mankind into a single entity.

[1921]

A Cliff Out of the Future

People sit or walk, hidden in patches of blind rays by luminous clouds of radiant silence, of radiant stillness.

Some of them are perched in high places, high in the air, in weightless chairs. Sometimes they paint, daubing away with their brushes. Whole companies of others carry round glass panels for floors and tables.

Other people walk on air with the help of walking sticks, or move swiftly through the air snow, moving over the surface of the cloud crust on skis of time. A great air-walk, an elevated highway crowded with skywalkers curves across the sky, above the poles of low towers for lightning compressed into coils. People move upon this weightless path as upon an invisible bridge. Either side is a sheer drop into the void; the path is marked by a thin black ribbon of earth.

Like a sea serpent swimming in the deep with its head raised high above the surface, a building appears, breasting the air as it swims, shaped like a reversed letter *L*. A flying serpent of a building. It swells like an iceberg in the Arctic Ocean.

A sheer glass cliff, a vertical street of dwellings, rising at an angle in the air, garbed in wind—a swan of these times.

People sit on the balconies of the building. They are gods of serene thought.

"The Second Sea is cloudless today."

"It is. Our great teacher of equality, the Second Sea above our heads; you must raise your hand to point it out. It extinguished the fire of states once pumps and fire hoses were attached to it. That was very hard to do back in those days. That was the great service the Second Sea has rendered us. As a sign of gratitude, man's face has been stamped on one of the clouds forever, a kind of postcard sent to a friend."

"The combat between the islands and the lands deprived of seacoasts has ended. We are all equally rich in seacoast, now that we have the Second Sea above us. But we were shortsighted then. The sands of stupidity had buried us in great mounds."

I sit here smoking a ravishing thought with an entrancing odor. A resinous sense of well-being enfolds my mind like a blanket.

We must never forget the moral duty every human owes to the citizens of his own body. To this complicated star built of bone.

Human consciousness governs these citizens, and must never forget that human happiness is the totality of the grains of sand of happiness of all those subject to its government. Let us always remember that every hair on a human head is a skyscraper, and from its windows thousands of Sashas and Mashas look out at the sun.

That is why sometimes just taking off your shirt or going for a swim in a creek in springtime is a source of more happiness than being the greatest man on earth. Taking off all your clothes to loaf on a beach, trying to turn back the receding sun—all that means you are letting daylight into the artificial night of your own internal government; tuning the strings of that government, of that great resonating soundboard, to the key of the sun.

You must not act like Arakcheev toward the citizens of your own bodies. Don't ever be afraid of lying naked in a sea of sunlight. Let's undress our bodies, and our cities as well. Let's give them glass armor to protect them from arrows of freezing weather.

Conversation across the way:

"Have you got any food matches?"

"Sure, let's light up and smoke our supper."

"Want some sweet smoke? Zig-zag brand?"

"Yes. These are imported from far away, from Continent A."

The edible smoke is superb, the patches of blue sky are enchanting. A quiet little star is locked in single combat with the bright blue sky.

Bodies are beautiful, once they are freed from the prison of clothes. Within them a pale blue dawn struggles with a milky one.

But the equation of human happiness was found and solved only after people understood that it twisted like a delicate hopvine around the trunk of the universe. To listen to the rustling of water reeds, to recognize the familiar eyes and soul of a friend in a crab at the seashore as it scuttles sideways, claws raised, always on the alert—something like this often gives us more happiness than all the things that bring us fame or the renown of, say, a military commander.

Human happiness is a secondary sound; it twists, turns around the fundamental sound of the universe.

Happiness is the pale moon circling the earths that go around the sun, circling the cow eyes of a little kitten as it scratches its ear, circling the coltsfoot in springtime, circling the splash of the sea waves.

These are the fundamental sounds of happiness, its wise fathers, the vibrating iron rod that antedates the family of voices. More simply, the axis of rotation. And this is the reason that city children cut off from nature are always unhappy, while for country children happiness is familiar and as inseparable as their shadows.

Man has taken the surface of Planet Earth away from the wise community of animals and plants and now he is lonely; he has no one to play tag or hide-and-seek with. In his empty room, surrounded by the darkness of nonbeing, there are no playmates and no games. Who can he play with? He is surrounded by an empty *no*. The souls of animals banished from their bodies have invaded him, and the plains of his being are now subject to their law.

They built animal cities in his heart.

Man seems to be choking to death on his own carbon.

His happiness was a printing press that lacked types of many numbers needed to print a reckoning: twos and threes; and without these numbers the Beautiful Program cannot be written. As animals fell into extinction, each took with him to the grave the private numbers of his species.

Whole sections of the account book of happiness had disappeared, like pages torn out of a manuscript. Twilight loomed on the horizon.

But a miracle happened: courageous minds have waked the sleeping soul of the sacred gray clay that covers the earth in layers, waked it as bread and meat. Earth has become edible, and every clay pit has become a table laid for dinner. The beautiful gift of the right to live has been given back to animals and plants.

And once more we are happy: a lion lies curled in my lap, asleep, and I sit here smoking my supper of air.

Khlebnikov (right) with Sergei Esenin and Anatoly Mariengof, Kharkov, 1920

Excerpt from The Tables of Destiny

Porfiry Krylov, drawing of Khlebnikov, 1922

It was in mathematics that Khlebnikov found his dominant metaphor. The presence of Time in poetic rhythm eventually forced him to look for the rhythms that sounded beneath the conventional ones, to seek meaning in the cyclical patterns of the universe. Number was the key. On February 25, 1911, the twenty-six-year-old poet wrote to his brother Alexander: "I am making a diligent study of numbers and have discovered quite a few patterns. I intend to keep going and work it all out completely, though, until I get some answers as to why it all behaves this way." That diligent study was to become almost an obsession, as Khlebnikov tried to work out an all-embracing system of correspondences between languages and the "language of the stars," between human behavior and the movement of the universe.

Khlebnikov traces the origins of this enterprise to the Russian defeat in the Russo-Japanese War. In a brief memoir written in 1919 he states: "I wanted to discover the reason for all those deaths." We come, then, to the perception that lies at the source of philosophical speculation and of all the great poetic structures of human culture. "I had not thought death had undone so many," Dante marvels. For Khlebnikov, trained as a mathematician, the free play of numbers offered the possibility of circumventing the disasters of history. To study the past in order to envisage the future is no new idea; what is new here, however, is the conception—unrelated to the cabalistic tradition—of numbers as the unifying force that creates, in some predictable way, the relationships within which we perceive meaning.

Khlebnikov tries to explain the subjective universe that we as human beings inhabit as a function of the objective universe of classical mathematics, a world of unique entities with inherent properties and fixed relationships among them: to make numbers explain and influence human behavior in the same way that human language does. He attempts to reconcile an abstract, self-contained system like mathematics with the human world of ambiguity and the pervasive presence of metaphor. His attempt, no matter how it may be judged objectively, is a powerful metaphoric act, an act of poetry on an awesome scale. And although poetry was his means to this attempted end, Khlebnikov is by no means a mystic. He saw himself rather as a prophet, a discoverer, in the line of Aryabkatta, Leibniz, Lomonosov, and Lobachevsky: thinkers with a vision of the whole, creators of new forms that would penetrate the surface of phenomena and yield a new art that might change the human condition.

In a wry little poem printed in 1914, Khlebnikov describes concisely the underlying principle of his view of history, the idea of an equilibrium produced by the shift from positive to negative states:

The law of the see-saw argues
That your shoes will be loose or tight,
That the hours will be day or night,
And the ruler of earth the rhinoceros
Or us.

It is this notion of an equilibrium to be found in a shift from positive to negative, from victory to disaster, that underlies The Tables of Destiny. *This work was to be Khlebnikov's crowning achievement. Like Poe's* Eureka, *it is a strange, seemingly "unpoetic" finale to a life's work. It was intended to document in seven sections—the first of those sections is translated here—the operation of this law of the see-saw, now called the Laws of Time.*

The Tables of Destiny

The fate of the Volga may serve as a lesson for the study of destiny. The day the Volga riverbed was sounded was the day of its subjugation, its conquest by the powers of sail and oar, the surrender of the Volga to mankind. The sounding of Destiny and a thorough study of its dangerous places should make its navigation a calm and easy matter, just as sailing the Volga became safe and easy once buoys with red and green lights marked the danger spots—the rocks, shoals, and sandbars of the river bottom. In the same way we can study the fissures and shifting shoals of Time.

Analogous soundings may be made in the stream of Time, establishing the laws of time past, and studying the channel of time to come; by sounding Destiny we proceed from the lessons of past centuries in order to arm the mind with new eyes, eyes of the intellect, that can make out events still in the distant future.

It has long been a commonplace that knowledge is a kind of power, and to foresee events is to be able to control them.

Here are two equations: one concerns and outlines the destiny of England; the other provides a basic time outline of India.

It is important to remember that in general opposed events—victory and defeat, beginning and end—are united in terms of powers of three (3^n). The number three is the wheel of death, as it were, for the initial event.

Moscow, January 16, 1922

"CROWNED WITH DAWNS"

A WAKE AT THE NEIGHBORS'
(THE HOUR OF BURIAL)

I discovered the pure Laws of Time in 1920 in Baku, the land of fire, in a tall building that housed the naval dormitory where I was living with Dobrokovsky. The exact date was December 17th.

A huge slogan "Dobrokuznia" was scrawled at an angle on the wall, a heap of brushes lay beside buckets of paint, and a constant refrain in my ears insisted that if someone named Nina would only show up, then out of the city of Baku would come the name of Bakunin. His enormous tattered shadow hung over us all. A sculptor began a bust of Columbus in a lump of green wax and unexpectedly produced a head of me. It was a good omen, a sign of good hope for someone sailing toward an unknown land, toward the continent of time. I wanted to find a key to the timepiece of humanity, to become humanity's watchmaker, and to map out a basis for predicting the future. All this took place in the land where man first encountered fire and tamed it into a domestic animal. In the land of fire—Azerbaidjan—fire changes its primordial appearance. It does not fall from heaven like a savage divinity, engendering fear; rather it rises from the earth like a gentle flower and almost begs us to pick it and tame it.

On the first day of spring in 1921 I went a supplicant to the eternal fires. Caught unawares at night by the fast-dropping twilight, I slept in the open steppe, on the bare ground, among clumps of grass and spiders' webs. The terrors of night surrounded me.

I discovered the equation for the inner zone of heavenly bodies of the solar system on September 25, 1920, at the Prolekult conference in Armavir, on the back benches of the meeting hall; during all the inflammatory business speeches, I computed the times of those stars in my notebook.

This equation for the first time fettered the stellar magnitudes together and made them subject to one general law, in tandem with the community of human beings.

I first resolved to search out the laws of time on the day after the battle of Tsushima, when news of the battle reached the Yaroslavl district where I was then living, in the village of Burmakino, at Kuznetsov's.

I wanted to discover the reason for all those deaths.

I remember springtime in the north country and the clink of bridle and stirrups; they used to make the horses trundle them across the fields in a special barrel, in order to give the rusty iron the silvery glitter of a new bridle and harness. The poor old horses in the north had to drag around a barrel filled with their own chains.

I had a true and reliable helper in my task—the chance encounter, in that famine of print, with the very book I could not do without.

It was an old gray mare, Comrade Graylegs, who gave me a chronicle of the events of 1917–1920; it was this that allowed me to begin calculating days, which was the next step.

I can still hear the panting breath of that traveling companion of mine.

I am firmly resolved, if these laws do not win a place among humans, to teach them to the enslaved race of horses. I have already expressed this firm resolution in a letter to Ermilov.

The first truths about space sought the force of social law in the surveyor's art, in order to determine the taxes upon circular or triangular plots, or to make an equitable division among the inheritors of a piece of land.

The first truths about time seek points of support for the equitable demarcation of generations, and transfer the desire for equity and law into a new dimension, that of time. But in this case as well the motivating force is that same old desire for equity, the division of time into equal time-estates.

Humanity, as a phenomenon caught up in the flow of time, was aware of the power of time's pure laws, but feelings of nationality were strengthened by recurring and opposed dogmas, all attempting to depict the essence of time with the paint of words.

Doctrines of good and evil, Ahriman and Ormuzd, eventual retribution—all these express the desire to speak of time before any measure for it was available, using only a bucket of paint.

And so the face of time was painted in words on the old canvases of the Koran, the Vedas, the Gospels, and other doctrines. That great face is adumbrated here also in the pure Laws of Time, but this time with the brush of number, and thus we take a different approach to the task of our predecessors. The canvas contains no words, only precise number, which functions here as the artist's brush stroke depicting the face of time.

Thus in the ancient task of the time-painter a certain shift has occurred.

Time-painting has abandoned the indeterminacy of words and now possesses an exact unit of measurement.

Those who think they can ignore the pure Laws of Time and still make correct judgments will seem like the old tyrant who had the ocean whipped because it destroyed his ships.

They would do better to study the laws of navigation.

First I discovered the characteristic reversibility of events after 3^5 days, 243 days. Then I continued to increase the powers and extents of the time-periods I had discovered, and began to apply them to the past of humanity.

That past suddenly became transparently clear; the simple law of time suddenly illuminated it in its entirety.

I understood then that time was structured in powers of two and three, the lowest possible even and odd numbers.

I understood that the true nature of time consists in the recurrent multiplication of itself by twos and threes, and when I recalled the old Slavic belief in the powers of "odd and even" I decided that wisdom was indeed a tree that grows from a seed. The superstition is all in the quotation marks.

Once I had uncovered the significance for time of odd and even, I had the sensation of holding in my hands a mousetrap in which aboriginal Fate quivered like a terrified little animal. The equations of time resemble a tree, simple as a treetrunk in their bases, and slender and complexly alive in the branches of their powers, where the brain and living soul of the equations are concentrated; they seem to be the reverse of equations of space, where the enormous number of the base is crowned by one, two, or three, but never anything further.

These were, I decided, two opposite movements within a single stretch of calculation.

I envisaged them very concretely: for space, I saw mountains, enormous stone masses as a base upon which the power perched like a bird of prey in repose, the bird of consciousness—compared to equations for time, which seemed like slender tree-trunks and flowering branches with living birds fluttering in them.

For space, time seemed an inflexible exponent; it could never be greater than three, while the base was alive and limitless; for time, on the contrary, the foundations were fixed as two and three, while the exponent lived a complex existence in the free play of values. Where I had previously been conscious of the empty steppes of time, there had suddenly sprung up orderly multinominals based on three and on two, and I felt like a traveler before whom suddenly appeared the crenelated walls and towers of a city no one even knew existed.

In the famous old legend, the city of Kitezh lay sunk in a deep dark lake in the forest, while here, out of each spot of time, out of every lake of time, arose an orderly multinominal of threes with towers and steeples, just like another Kitezh.

Series such as $1053 = 3^{3+3} + 3^{3+2} + 3^{3+1}$, where the number of members is the same as the base number, the exponent of the leading power is twice three, and the other exponents diminish by one, or the well-known number $365 = 3^5 + 3^4 + 3^3 + 3^2 + 3^1 + 3^0 + 1$, have on the one hand disclosed the ancient relationship of the year to the days and on the other hand have given a new meaning to the old legend of the city of Kitezh.

A city of threes with its towers and steeples rings loudly from out of the depths of time. An orderly city with numerical towers has replaced previous visions of spots of time.

I did not dream up these laws: I simply took the live magnitudes of time, tried to divest myself of existing notions, to see what were the laws by which these magnitudes changed one into the other, and constructed equations based on the experience. And one after the other, the numerical expressions for magnitudes of time revealed a strange kinship with the expressions for space, at the same time that they moved in a reverse direction.

Number is a cup into which we may pour the liquid of any magnitude whatsoever, while the equation is a device that yields a string of magnitudes where the fixed numbers are the motionless nuts of the equation, its framework, and the magnitudes *m* and *n* are the mobile elements of the contrivance, the wheels, levers, and flywheels of the equation.

In my mind I would occasionally compare the numbers in an equation whose magnitudes were fixed with the skeleton of a body, and the magnitudes *m* and *n* with the muscles and flesh of a body, the whole suddenly brought to life like animals in a fairytale.

In the equation I distinguished muscular structure from bone.

And behold, equations of time appeared as mirror images of equations of space.

Equations of space came to resemble extinct fossilized animals with huge skeletons and tiny skulls: the brain is the crown of the body.

If the expression for volume is A^3, A here can increase to infinity, but the exponent will always be three.

Three is the fixed magnitude, the bone of the equation; A is its liquid part. For two inverse points in time the expression $3^a + 3^a$ or $3^n + 3^n$ (or simply 3^n) is very distinctive. Such a time-expression unites event and counterevent in time.

An event of movement A and its reverse $-A$: here the fixed base is three and the infinitely increasing exponent is *n*—isn't this a reverse flow of the computation?

What the ancient doctrines spoke of, what they threatened in the name of vengeance, now becomes the cruel and simple force of this equation; its dry language contains all the force of "Vengeance is mine, and I shall repay" and the terrible, unforgiving Jehovah of the ancients.

Indeed, the law of Moses and the entire Koran is very probably contained in the iron force of this equation.

But think how much ink we save! What a rest for the inkwell! In this we see the growth of progress through the centuries. With the colors of blood, iron, and death we can adorn the phantasmal outlines of the expression for $3x$ days.

Behavior and punishment, act and retribution.

Say the victim dies at the initial point.

The killer will die after 3^5.

Suppose the initial point was a step of conquest, marked by a major military success for some wave of humanity. Then the second point, after 3^n days, will mark an end to that movement, the day of its rebuff, a day that shouts: Whoa! Stop! Even though all during these 3^n days the whip of fate kept cracking to shouts of: Hey! Giddyap! Forward!

So the day of the battle of Mukden, February 26, 1905, which stopped the Russian advance to the East, an advance that began with the taking of Isker by Yermak and his band, occurred $3^{10} + 3^{10} = 2 \times 3^{10}$ after the taking of Isker on October 26, 1581.

The battle of Angora on July 20, 1402, which established a limit, a fixed threshold to the western push of the Mongols, occurred 3^{10} after the Tatars' enormous success, their conquest of Kiev on December 6, 1240, which marked the beginning of the approach of the East, when the East turned to the West and removed its warlike visor.

The battle of Kulikovo Field, August 26, 1380, stopped the westward drive of the Eastern populations, those waves of Huns, Slavs, Magyars, Polovtsians, Pechenegs, and Tatars. But it occurred $3^{11} + 3^{11} = 2 \times 3^{11}$ after the sack of Rome by Alaric on August 24, 410, when Rome was burned to the ground. The taking of Constantinople in 1453 by the Turks set limits to the ancient Greek drive to the East. But this event, the fall of the Greek capital, happened $3^{11} \times 4$ after the year 487 B.C., when the Greeks had conquered the Persians and surged into the East.

The Roman drive toward the East began around the year 30 B.C., when Rome became master of the Mediterranean and subjugated the Eastern capital, Alexandria (August 4, 30, the taking of Alexandria by Octavian).

That year marked the full flowering of Rome, the essential step toward the East; 3^{11} days later brought the year 455 (July 12, 455), the year of Rome's fall and destruction.

The East shattered its opponent's sword: Bulgaria was conquered by the Turks at the battle of Trnovo on July 17, 1393; 3^{11} days later a reverse event occurred: she was declared independent by the treaty of Berlin on July 13, 1878. Here the law of 3^n unites the point of enslavement, of hands in chains, and the point of independence.

Let us now demonstrate our truth, that an event upon reaching an age of 3^n days changes its sign to the reverse (the yes-integer factor as an indicator of direction gives place to a no-integer factor [+1 and −1]), that upon completion of the time sequence represented by the numerical structure 3^n events stand in the same relation to each other as two trains proceeding in opposite directions along the same track, by means of the modest powers of *n*.

The large exponents are concerned with the dance and drift of states, their baton controls the great hopak of invasions and movements of peoples; while the small ones concern the lives of separate individuals, controlling them by means of retribution or by shifts in the structure of society, translating into numbers the ancient original, the old tables written in the language of words: "Vengeance is mine, and I will repay."

So the military agent Min put down the Moscow uprising on December 26, 1905; he was killed 3^5, 243 days later, on August 26, 1906.

The avenging hand of Konopliannikova, or Fate itself, pulled the trigger of the revolver that shot him.

Autocrat Nikolai Romanov was shot on July 16, 1918, $3^7 + 3^7$ after he dissolved the Duma on July 22, 1906.

The American president Garfield was killed on July 2, 1881, 3^5 days after his election to the post on November 2, 1880.

The attempt upon the life of the governor-general of Poland, Count Berg, took place 243 days after the beginning of the uprising; in other words, Judgment Day, the day of vengeance, took place 3^5 after the event that called for that vengeance.

The freedom fighter Robert Blum was executed on November 9, 1848, 3^5 days after the beginning of the 1848 uprising (March 13, 1848).

The tsarist government's debts were recognized by Soviet Russia on November 6, 1921, $3^6 + 3^6 = 1458$ days after the beginning of Soviet power on November 10, 1917, when they had been declared null and void.

The Miliukov–Kerensky government of March 10, 1917,

was set up 3^5 days before the government of Lenin and Trotsky on November 10, 1917.

The defeat of Wrangel, Kolchak's successor, and the end of the civil war occurred on November 15, 1920, 3^6 days after Kolchak's proclamation of himself as "provisional head of state" on November 17, 1918.

The abandonment of the front line by the troops and the disbanding of military units on December 7, 1917, occurred 3^5 days after Miliukov's declaration on April 9, 1917, about "war to the end" and loyalty to the Allied Powers.

Universal Education Day, August 11, 1918, occurred $3^5 + 2^2$ days after the Tolstoyan mood of the period of troop disbandment on December 7, 1917.

The English struck at the Continent 3^n days after the battle of Hastings, when their island was invaded by an army from the Continent.

The battle of Hastings, which represented the victory of Continent over Island, took place on October 3, 1066; the indigenous population was totally defeated, the island occupied by hordes of Danes; $3^9 + 3^9$ days later occurred the battle of Glenville, when the English defeated the French on June 13, 1174.

3^{10} days later occurred the naval battle of Bornholm, July 22, 1227, when the English avenged themselves on the Danes by defeating their recent conquerors. The island was avenged. Thus in turn were the French and the Danes defeated at sea 3^n days after the reverse event—the defeat of the English.

Thus do *yes* and *no* constantly reverse themselves.

We have seen the military duel of East and West; we have seen how the sword falls from the hands of one of the two combatants 3^n days after a successful attack, when one or another capital city is turned to rubble and ashes.

Isker, Kiev, Rome, London form one series. The battles of Mukden, Angora, Kulikovo Field, and Bornholm resounded 3^n days after the first series.

Threshold, obstacle, and stoppage were put to movement; victory is given to the conquered, destruction to the conqueror. The event makes a turn of *2d*, two right angles, and forms a negative turning point of time. The midnight of the event becomes its noonday and reveals the regular working of the time-pieces of humanity, ticking in the capital cities of states long blown to dust.

Those who have no ordinary watch, would do well to wear the great timepiece of humanity and pay heed to its regular movements, its tick-tick-tick.

After a lapse of time of 3^n days the second event moves counter to the first, in reverse, like a train speeding in the opposite direction, threatening to derail the purpose of the first event.

The "truth" is, and we put the word in quotation marks for those who still care to doubt it, that events are spatially determined; specifically, the direction of motion of a force becomes a dependent variable of the count of days, that is to say the natural quantities of time. Here we have a quantitative connection, discovered through experiment, between the principles of time and space. The first bridge between them.

It derives from a careful study of the live quantities of time and the law of numbers by which these quantities convert one into another.

If we compare the live natural volumes of blocks of wood with right-angled and equal sides, these volumes will convert one into another according to the law of A^3 or n^3, where n or A is the length of a side according to the law of volumes, then the exponent 3 (a fixed number, fettering the quantities) is the solid bottom and fixed banks of the equation, while the base A is the moving water, the flow of the equation, and any quantity whatsoever may be proposed for it: A is the river of the equation.

For the law of live areas, by which areas merge one into the other, the relation A^2, n^2 applies, and here the fixed number is 2.

Quantities of time, however, merge into each other according to a law of 3^n days and 2^n days: here we have an unrestricted exponent, free as the wind, and a restricted base, the 3 or 2.

The river of the equation flows through the powers, and its banks are the base: 3 = a fixed number, while n is free and may be any possible number.

The delightful notion occurs that in fact there is no time and no space; there are only two different ways of counting, two inclines to the same roof, two paths through a single edifice of numbers.

Time and space together seem to comprise a single tree of mathematics, but in one case the imaginary squirrel of calculation moves from the branches to the base, in the other from the base to the branches.

These operations on quantities demonstrate the art of determining the greatest possible equality by means of the smallest possible inequality.

How many centuries would it take to determine (write out) a number, where a column of three 3s is the exponent of a 3, counting by tens?

Whereas here we are able to define it in an instant, extracting it from the sequence of others, by having recourse to equalities of a higher order.

We might call this the law of the least consumption of ink, the "ink-conservation" principle.

The impulse to find the smallest possible numbers is another law, a kind of Nirvana, the teachings of Buddha in the realm of numbers.

In the calculation that time makes, a gravitation to the numbers that surround the world of nothing (that is, one, two, and three) determines the structure of the base; its fixed bases are threes and twos. In spatial equations three, two, and one are the exponents.

And the base, on the contrary, goes to infinity.

Could we possibly refer to time as space turned upside down?

Raising to a power represents extreme economy in the use of ink; a succession of centuries can be written out (extracted from a sequence of others) with two or three strokes of a pen. This art lies at the foundation of both spatial calculation and the calculation of time.

But where space is concerned, it is the exponent that is created by the propensity toward the smallest possible numbers, the greatest proximity to zero; in the case of time it is the base.

Spatial quantities

	In the base	In the exponent
The constraint of three or two		X
Infinite increase of the number (numerical freedom)	X	

For time

	In the base	In the exponent
Two or three constrained	X	
Infinite increase of the number		X

In other words, space and time are two inverse directions of the same calculation, that is M^n and N^m.

In the lives of individuals I have noticed an especially turbulent time-period with the structure 2^{13} and 13^2. It calls forth triumphs beneath the sign of Mars or Venus, it doesn't matter which.

So Boris Samorodov who raised the revolt on the White ships in the Caspian, did so $2^{13} + 13^2$ days after his birth.

As I see it, the spirit of courageous deeds was called up in him by two to the thirteenth power, counting from his birth.

If indeed the pure Laws of Time exist, then they must govern without distinction everything that is subject to the flow of time, be it the soul of Gogol, Pushkin's *Eugene Onegin,* the planets of the solar system, shifts in the earth's crust, the terrible change from the kingdom of reptiles to the kingdom of men, from the Devonian era to an era marked by the interference of man in the life and structure of Planet Earth.

In fact, in the equation $x = 3^n + 3^n$, the interval of time for negative shifts, if we make $n = 11$, then x will equal the time between the destruction of Rome in 410 by peoples from the East, and the battle of Kulikovo Field, which put an end to the advance of those same peoples, a rebuff to the East. If we let

$n = 10$, we get x equal to the time between Yermak's expedition and the retreat of Kuropatkin: these points represent the beginning and the end of Russian penetration of the East.

If we let $n = 18$, we get the time between the Tertiary age and our own. And, finally, if $n = 23$, then $x = 369, 697, 770$ years, or the interval between the earth's Devonian age when reptiles were the lords of creation and the present day, when the Earth is a book with the shrieking title "Man." And does not this secret language based on three serve to explain the superstitious terror that man feels for reptiles, our frequently inoffensive enemies?

Between the Devonian age and our own, according to the determinations of Professor Holmes, there has elapsed a period of $3^{3^3-2^2} + 3^{3^3-2^2}$ days or $3^{23} + 3^{23}$ days.

That period of time marks the change from the domination of glitter-scaled reptiles to the domination of naked man in his soft envelope of skin. Only the hair on his head, like a wind blowing from centuries gone by, recalls his past. Considered from this perspective, people can be thought of as anti-reptiles. The crawlers on the ground were replaced by human beings, who fall and rebound constantly, like a ball. According to the pure laws of time, whose herald and trumpeter I hereby announce myself, both the life of the earth's crust and shifts in the structure of human society are equally subject to the very same equations.

Here is the law of English sea power: $x = k + 3^9 + 3^9n + (n-1)(n-2)2^{16} - 3^{9n-2}$, where $k =$ the day in 1066 when the island was conquered by the Danes at the Battle of Hastings. If $n = 1$, then x falls on the year 1174, the year of the struggle with France; if $n = 2$, then x comes out as 1227, the year of the struggle with Denmark; if $n = 3$, then x comes out as 1588, the year of the Spanish Armada.

All these wars guaranteed to Albion domination of the seas. And this was indeed to have been expected, because the equation is built on the base of three, and its initial point was an English defeat.

Day unit	*In years*	
	Taking a year equal to 365 days	*Taking a year equal to 365 1/4 days*
2^0 = 1		
2^1 = 2		
2^2 = 4		
2^3 = 8		
2^4 = 16		
2^5 = 32		
2^6 = 64		
2^7 = 128		
2^8 = 256	a year minus 109 days	a year minus 109 days
2^9 = 512	1 year and 147 days	1 year and 147 days
2^{10} = 1024	3 years minus 71 days	3 years minus 72 days
2^{11} = 2048	6 years minus 142 days	6 years minus 143 days
2^{12} = 4096	11 years and 81 days	11 years and 79 days
2^{13} = 8192	22 years and 162 days	22 years and 157 days
2^{14} = 16,384	45 years minus 41 days	45 years minus 52 days
2^{15} = 32,768	90 years minus 82 days	90 years minus 104 days
2^{16} = 65,536	179 years and 201 days	179 years and 156 days
2^{17} = 131,072	359 years and 37 days	359 years minus 53 days
2^{18} = 262,144	718 years and 74 days	718 years minus 106 days
2^{19} = 524,209	1436 years and 148 days	1436 years minus 212 days
2^{20} = 1,048,576	2872 years and 296 days	

Day unit	*In years*	
3^0 = 1		
3^1 = 3		
3^2 = 9		
3^3 = 27		
3^4 = 81		
3^5 = 243		
3^6 = 729	2 years minus 1 day	2 years minus 2 days
3^7 = 2187	6 years minus 3 days	6 years minus 4 days

Day unit	*In years*	
$3^8 = 6561$	18 years minus 9 days	18 years minus 13 days
$3^9 = 19{,}683$	54 years minus 27 days	54 years minus 40 days
$3^{10} = 59{,}049$	161 years and 284 days	161 years and 244 days
$3^{11} = 177{,}147$	485 years and 122 days	485 years and 1 day
$3^{12} = 531{,}441$	1456 years and 1 day	1455 years and 2 days
$3^{13} = 1{,}594{,}323$	4368 years and 3 days	4365 years
$3^{14} = 4{,}782{,}969$	13,104 years and 9 days	

The life of centuries in the light of 3^n.

The eternal duel, illuminated by the torches of 3^n.

The staff of victory changes hands, passed from one warrior to another.

Waves of two worlds, the alternating spears of East and West, clashing through the centuries.

March 5, 3313 B.C. The conquest of India by the Aryans. A wave of Whites from the West.	$3^{13} + 3^7 - 2 \times 3^5$	November 10, 1256 Conquest of Baghdad by the Mongols under Hulagu; a wave of Mongols pouring from the East.
August 24, 410 Alaric sacks Rome, the capital of the West. A wave from the East pours into the West.	$3^{11} + 3^{11}$	August 24, 1380 The battle of Kulikovo; it acts as a dam against the people from the East; East meets with a rebuff.
July 2, 451 The rout of Attila, rebuff to the East.	$3^{12} - 2^7$	February 26, 1905 The battle of Mukden, rebuff to the East.

October 26, 1581 Yermak conquers Isker, the capital of Siberia. A wave against the East.	$3^{10} + 3^{10}$	February 26, 1905 The battle of Mukden, a halt to the Russian advance to the East.
September 3, 36 B.C. The battle of Naulochus, Roman wave in the West.	$3^{19} + 3^{11}$	September 26, 1904 The battle of Shakha, a halt to the West.

Let us make the bones of these times speak; let us clothe them with the flesh of human life and grant to the cliffs of time the voice of events in $3^n + 3^n$ days.

August 24, 410 Alaric takes Rome; a wave from the East against the West.	$3^{11} + 3^{11}$	August 26, 1380 The battle of Kulikovo Field; a halt to the peoples of the East.
October 26, 1581 Yermak takes Isker; a Russian wave against the East.	$3^{10} + 3^{10}$	February 26, 1905 The battle of Mukden, rebuff to Russia.
October 3, 1066 The battle of Hastings; subjugation of England.	$3^9 + 3^9$	June 13, 1174 The battle of Glenville; island England defeats the Continent.
May 18, 1899 The Hague peace conference of kings.	3^8	May 9, 1917 The peace proposal of labor at the Petrograd Soviet of Workers' Deputies.
July 22, 1906 The state Duma dissolved by order of Nikolai Romanov.	$3^7 + 3^7$	July 16, 1918 Nikolai Romanov is executed.

November 1, 1917 Beginning of Soviet power in Russia.	$3^6 + 3^6$	November 7, 1921 A shift to the right, negotiations concerning the assumption of Russia's debts.
December 26, 1905 Uprising in Moscow, put down by Min.	3^5	August 26, 1906 Min assassinated by Konopliannikova.
May 21, 1792 The king deals with foreign powers.	3^4	August 10, 1792 The taking of the royal palace.

The 19th century in the flaring torchlight of 2^n days and 3^n days.

The growth of events after 2^{14} days.

June 19, 1815 Waterloo, a rebuff for the West. Victory of the Eastern half of the continent over the Western half.	$2^{15} - 3^2$	February 26, 1905 Mukden, a second rebuff to the West. The direction of the event is exactly the same. Victory for the East.
"The little mailed fist of Germany" in 1870. September 2, 1870 = Sedan. 2^{14} days later Bismarck's winged words about "blood and iron" began to fly like zeppelins, and like the teeth of the magic dragon became a war in the air, on sea and land, underground and underwater; they hissed across the trenches like a poisoned wind, like exhalations of death.	2^{14}	"The big mailed fist of Germany," July 11, 1915, world war. Germany's iron fist, which once threatened only France, now threatens the whole of Planet Earth.

November 14, 1860 The taking of Peking (the sea-peoples beseige the continent of Asia).	2^{14}	September 23, 1905 The Russo-Japanese War. Second victory for the sea. The Continent is conquered.

Zangezi

Pyotr Miturich, bathhouse at Santalovo, 1922, where Khlebnikov died

Khlebnikov manipulates conventional poetic forms in surprising ways. Basic to his style is the notion of what he called a "supersaga"—a number of seemingly discrete texts put together to form a whole. Zangezi *is the most extraordinary of these strange hybrids, "an architecture composed of narratives," as Khlebnikov puts it in his introduction.*

The supersaga works against the notion of the discreteness of a particular composition; it points to the fact of any artist's work as a continuous on-going whole, a constant reconsideration of a few basic themes. It also makes us reexamine our sense of the way things hang together, the way we as readers make sense of a text. The apparent difficulties of a text like Zangezi*—unexplained references, seemingly illogical and nonsensical juxtapositions—are deliberate attempts by its author to create a text where our experience of the world will not serve, but where we are forced, as children are, to perceive an unknown world.*

Khlebnikov valued the writing of children; in their work he saw human creativity before reason and intelligence had been at work, before the oppositions skill–clumsiness and good–bad are learned. In the innocence of such work Khlebnikov thought he could make out the quality of what all writing would be like "in the Future," when these oppositions and um, *the dualistic reasoning power that creates them, have dissolved. His own use of alogical, primitive, nonrational "languages" attempts to recapture the childhood experience, the creation of a new world, the discovery of new continents.*

The hero of Khlebnikov's theater piece, his alter ego, is the prophet Zangezi, conceived somewhat in the spirit of Nietzsche's Zarathustra. Like the young Khlebnikov—and like those other young forest heros, Hiawatha and Siegfried—Zangezi understands the language of the birds. But he understands the powers of language in its broadest senses—and the various "planes" of Zangezi *catalogue and exem-*

plify some of the possible languages that connect the universe: the language of the gods, the beyonsense language zaum, *the language of the stars in Plane Eight, where each letter and sound of the alphabet is in fact an arrangement of points in space ("Alphabet is the echo of space!"), the declension of intellect in Plane Nine, sound-writing in Plane Fifteen, fragments of popular speech in Planes Sixteen and Seventeen, the grand movement of numbers as history in Planes Eighteen and Nineteen, and finally, in Plane Twenty, in a pure theatrical metaphor, a scene from some fantastic medieval morality play, the crystallization of all human endeavor in the struggle of Laughter with Death.*

Zangezi *was printed in 1922, shortly before Khlebnikov's death, and it was produced in May 1923 at the Museum of Artistic Culture in Petrograd, designed, staged, and performed by Khlebnikov's friend Vladimir Tatlin.*

Zangezi *is in many ways Khlebnikov's summation of his own work. It is a presentation of his ideas and poetic style joined in an edifice like some fabulous cathedral, whose bewildering juxtapositions of mosaics and frescoes will tell, if they are read correctly, the story of a transcendent faith in the human spirit.*

Zangezi
A Supersaga in Twenty Planes

INTRODUCTION

A story is made of words, the way a building is made of construction units. Equivalent words, like minute building blocks, serve as the construction units of a story.

A superstory, or supersaga, is made up out of independent sections, each with its own special god, its special faith, and its special rule. To the old Muscovite question about one's orthodoxy, "How dost thou believe?", each section must answer independently of its neighbor. Each is free to confess its own particular faith. The building block of the supersaga, its unit of construction, is the first-order narrative. The supersaga resembles a statue made from blocks of different kinds of stone of varying colors—white for the body, blue for the cloak and garments, black for the eyes.

It is carved from the varicolored blocks of the Word, each with its own different structure. Thus do we discover a new kind of operation in the realm of verbal art. Narrative is architecture composed of words; an architecture composed of narratives is a "supersaga."

The artist's building block is no longer the word, but the first-order narrative.

A STACK OF WORD PLANES

(The mountains. At the edge of a clearing rises a steep craggy rock; it resembles an iron needle seen through a magnifying glass. Like a pilgrim's staff left standing against a wall, it stands against perpendicular slopes of layers of rock overgrown by the pine forest. A bridge-platform connects it to the bedrock, the re-

sult of a landslide that has fallen across the top of the crag like a straw hat. This platform is Zangezi's favorite place. He comes here every morning to recite his poems.

Here he reads his sermons to the people or to the forest. Beside the crag an enormous fir tree moves its heavy branches like blue waves; it hides part of the crag as if befriending and protecting it.

Here and there sheets of the bedrock have pushed their way above ground, black surfaces among the roots. These are the corners of stone books read by the dwellers beneath the earth, and roots lie twisted in great knots wherever they appear.

The sound of a pine forest in the wind.

Pillows of reindeer moss, silvered by the dew. Night weeps as she passes here.

Among the tree trunks stand living black stones, like the dark bodies of giants on their way to war.)

PLANE ONE: THE BIRDS

(These are the birds' morning speeches to the rising sun.)

Chaffinch (from the very top of the fir tree, puffing out its silver throat) Peet páte tveechan! Peet pate tveechan! Peets páte tveechan!

Yellow Bunting (quietly, from the top of a walnut tree) Kree-tee-tee-tee-tee-ee—tsuey-tsuey-tsuey-sssueyee.

Tree Swallow Vyer-vyór véeroo syek-syek-syek! Ver-ver véeroo sek-sek-sék!

Mountain Sparrow Tyortee yedéegredee (*he sees people and hops into the tall fir tree*). Tyortée yedeegredee!

Yellow Bunting (rocking back and forth on a branch) Tsuey-tsuey-tsuey-sssueyée.

Green Chiff-Chaff (alone, flitting over the green sea of the pine grove, grazing waves that the wind keeps forever in motion) Prúeyn! ptseerép-ptseerép! Ptséerep!—tsehsehséh.

Yellow Bunting Tsuey-suey-suey-ssuéy (*rocks back and forth on a twig*).

Blue Jay Pe̋eoo! Pe̋eoo! pyak, pyak, pyák!

Barn Swallow Tseeve̋ets! Tseeze̋ets!

Black-Banded Warbler Behbot éh-oo-véhvyats!

Cuckoo Koo-kőo! koo-koo! (*rocks back and forth on a treetop*).

(*Silence. A young birdcatcher passes, with a cage on his back.*)

PLANE TWO: THE GODS

(*Little by little, the mist clears. Sheer cliff faces appear: they resemble the faces of men who have led harsh, uncompromising lives; clearly, this is the nesting place of the gods. Swanwings hover upon transparent bodies, and the grasses murmur and bend beneath invisible footsteps. And in truth, the gods are at hand! Louder and louder their voices resound; this is the assembly of the gods of all nations, their great gathering, their encampment in the mountains.*

Tien stands; his long hair touches the ground; it forms his only garment. With a flat iron he smoothes away wrinkles.

Shang-ti wipes from his face the soot of Western cities. "Little better so, maybe." Two snowy wisps of hair, like little rabbits, perch above his ears. He has a long Chinese moustache.

White Juno is draped in green hopvines: she scrapes at her snow-white shoulder with a diligent metal file, cleaning scales from the white stone.

Unkulunkulu listens attentively to the sound of a beetle tunneling its way through the beam of his wooden body.)

Eros Mara-róma
Be̋ebah-bőol
Oook, kooks, ell!
Redede̋edee dee-dee-de̋e!
Pe̋eree, pépee, pa-pa-pe̋e!
Chógi, gőona, géni-gan

Ahl, Ell, Eeell!
Ahlee, Ellee, Eelee!
Ek, ak, oook!
Gamch, gemch, ee-ó!
rrr-pee! rrr-pee!

The Gods Respond Na-no-na!
Echee, oochee, ochee
Kézee, nézee, dzee-ga-gá!
Neezaréézee ozeeréé
Mayahmóóra zeemoró!
Peeps!
Mazacheecheecheemoro!
Plyan!

Veles Broovoo róó roo roo róó!
Péétse tsápe seh seh séh!
Broovoo róóroo roo-roo-róó!
Séétsee, léétsee tsee-tsee-tséé!
Painch, panch, painnch!

Eros Emch, amch, oomch!
Dóómchee dámchee dómchee,
Makaráko keeochérk!
Tseetseeleetsee tsee-tsee-tséé!
Kookaréékee keekeekóó.
Rééchee chééchee tsee-tsee-tséé.
Olga, Elga, Alga.
Peets, patch, pótch! Ekhamchéé!

Juno Peerarára peerooróóroo!
Layo lólo Booaroh-óh
Beechehólo seh-seh-séh.
Béchee! Béechee! éébee béé!
Zeezazééza eezazó!
Eps, Aps, Eps!
Móóree-góóree reekokó!
Mio, Máo, Moom!
Ep!

Unkulunkulu Rapr, grapr, apr! zhai!
Kaf! Bzuey! Kaf!
Zhrap, gap, bokv kook
Rrrtoopt! Toopt!

(The gods rise up into the air. Once more the mist thickens and burns blue upon the rockface.)

PLANE THREE: THE PEOPLE

(From a stack of varicolored word blocks.)

The People Goddam, what a climb!

First Passerby So this is the place? This is where your fool of the forest appears?

Second Passerby This is the place.

First Passerby What does he do?

Second Passerby He reads, he talks, he breathes, he sees, he hears, he walks up and down. Mornings he prays.

First Passerby Who to?

Second Passerby Nobody can tell. Maybe to the flowers. Or the bugs. Or the toads in the woods.

First Passerby He's an idiot! A fool! The sermons of a forest fool! What about cows? Does he at least keep a herd of cows?

Second Passerby Not so far. And look! See how clear the path is? There's not a blade of grass left growing anywhere around. People are constantly coming up here, see? They've beaten a path right to the cliff.

First Passerby He's weird! But let's listen, at least.

Second Passerby He's kind of cute. Almost feminine. But he won't last long.

First Passerby Why, is it beginning to get to him?

Second Passerby Yes. (*People pass.*)

Third Passerby There he is up there, and down here below, all these people . . . What are they, some sort of spitoon for the spittle of his wisdom?

First Passerby Maybe they're all drowning in it. They swim around, they swallow and choke . . .

Second Passerby Have it your way. What's he supposed to be then, some kind of lifesaver?

First Passerby Exactly! A lifesaver thrown from the sky.

First Passerby And so here begins the wisdom of the forest fool. Teacher! Here we are! We're listening!

Second Passerby Wait a minute, what's this? A piece of Zangezi's writing by the root of this pinetree, stuck in a fieldmouse's hole. The handwriting is very beautiful.

First Passerby Well? Read it! Read it out loud!

PLANE FOUR

Second Passerby (he reads) "The Tables of Destiny! I carve you in letters of black night, you Tables of Destiny!

Three numbers! Just like myself in youth, myself in old age, myself in middle age. Let us follow the dusty road together.

$10^5 + 10^4 + 11^5 = 742$ years and 34 days. Read, eyes, the law of the downfall of empires:

Behold the equation: $x = k + n(10^5 + 10^4 + 11^5) - [10^2 - (2n-1)\,11]$ days.

k = the moment of reckoning in time, the rush of the Romans into the East, the battle of Actium. Egypt yields to Rome. This occurred on September 2, 31 B.C.

If $n = 1$, the value of x in the equation of the downfall of nations will be as follows: x = July 21, A.D. 711, or the day of proud Spain's defeat at the hands of the Arabs.

Proud Spain has fallen!

If $n = 2$, x = May 29, 1453.

The hour has struck: Constantinople is taken by the savage Turks. The city of the Caesars drowns in blood, and

Turkish bagpipes howl their savage delight. Osman rides roughshod over the corpse of the second Rome. The green cloak of the Prophet hangs in blue-eyed Sophia's sanctuary.

On big-bellied horses the victors ride, with bedsheets wound about their heads.

The song of the three wings of destiny: Kind to some, terrible to others! The integer one abandons the five and joins the ten, abandons the wing and joins the wheel, and the movements of the number in three frames (10^5, 10^4, 11^5) are fixed by the equation.

Between the fall of Persia on October 1, 331 B.C. beneath the spear of Alexander the Great and the fall of Rome beneath the mighty blows of Alaric on August 24, 410, there elapsed a period of 741 years, or $10^5 + 11^5 + 10^4 - [3^6 + 1]/2 - 2^3 \times 3^2$ days.

The Tables of Destiny! Read them, read them, you Passersby! Number-warriors will pass before you like projections filmed in different segments of time, in different planes of time, and the sum of all their bodies, their various ages added together, equals the block of time between the downfalls of empires that had once been mighty and threatening."

Second Passerby Obscure. None too comprehensible, either. And yet—the lion's claw is visible in all of this! You can sense its presence somehow! A scrap of paper, and on it engraved the fates of nations for someone possessed of superior vision!

PLANE FIVE: WORDS

Changara Zangezi has come! Speechmaker! Speak to us! We hear you. Our souls are a floor beneath your feet. Brave comer! We believe in you, we await you. Our eyes, our souls—we are a floor beneath your feet, Unknowable!

An Oriole Feeo éhoo.

PLANE SIX

Zangezi I have come like a butterfly
Into the hall of human life,
And must spatter my dusty coat
As signature across its bleak windows,
As a prisoner scratches his name
On fate's unyielding windowpane.
Human life is papered thick
With grayness and boredom!
The transparent NO of its windows!
Already I have worn away
My bright blue glow, my pointillated patterns,
My wing's blue windstorm. The bright motes
Of my first freshness are gone, my wings waver,
Colorless and stiff. I droop despairing
At the windows of the human world.
Numbers, eternal numbers, sound in the beyond;
I hear their distant conversation. Number
Calls to number; number calls me home.

Second Passerby He wants to be a butterfly, he thinks he's so smart, that's what he wants to be.

Third Passerby A pretty poor prophet, if you ask me. A butterfly? He looks more like an old lady!

Believers Recite us some of your self-sounding poems! Tell us the story of *L*!

Speak to us in that beyonsense language of yours! Describe the horrors of our age in the words of Alphabet! So that never again will we have to see war between peoples, the sabers of Alphabet; instead let us hear the crash of Alphabet's long spears, the fight of the hostile forces *R* and *L*, *K* and *G!*

The terror of the plumes in their helmets! The terror of their spears! The awful outlines of their faces: wild and wistful, full of sunburnt space! In those days the very skin of nations was eaten by the moths of civil war, and capital cities crumbled like stale bread. The dew of human kindness had vanished into air.

We have heard of *L*. We know it is the sudden halt of a falling point upon a broad transverse plane. We know about *R;* we know it is the point that penetrates, that cuts like a razor through the transverse plane. *R* rips and resonates, ravages boundaries, forms rivers and ravines.

Alphabet is the echo of space.

Tell us!

PLANE SEVEN

Zangezi You tell me the Ruriks are dead, the Romanovs are dead,
Kaledins and Krymovs, Kornilovs and Kolchaks have fallen—
No! The landlords' defenders have clashed with their slaves,
Kiev has fallen twenty times over, twenty times taken
And trampled to dust.
The rich man wept and the poor man laughed
When Kaledin put a bullet through his brain.
The Constituent Assembly faltered.
Darkness filled the empty stronghold—
No, the "hold" is broken off in a howl,
A dying breath, a choking forth, and the mouth grows cold.
The hour of *K* has come!
Upon a cloud of power, the cogs of *L*.
Where is your age-old dishonor, *L?*
L—underground hermit of all ages!
Citizen of the mousehole, the typhoon of time
Rushes upon you—days, hours, months, years—in pilgrimage.
The weather changes—*L* days are upon us!
L, the sweet light of laziness, of love and languor!
In "living multitudes" you lull us twice.
All nations bowed before you
When the great war ended.
R, Rah, Roh! Tra-ra-ra!

Rasp of rapaciousness, insatiable war's ha-ha.
Rattling claptrap, rushing on rails
Forged in the fires of Scandinavia.
Like shaken canvas you roared over Russia,
Carrying south
The metallic clacket of wagon wheels.
Overnights of obdurate snowfall, havering the heart.
The mouse's body racked by the claws of the cold.
The rogue back of the wind-horse bore you across Russia.
And villages over the countryside all called out:
   Come see us!
Rattling claptrap!
Destroying delight, you forgot about obstacle,
And in the distance stood *G,* a rod broken in twain.
R in the hands of *L!*
Imagine an eagle, austerely unfurling its angling wings,
   Longing for Lel—for lull and loll,
Then *R* flies off like a pea from the pod
   And abandons the word Russia.
Imagine a nation become like a stricken deer,
Imagine it raked and raw in the flanks,
Imagine it move like a deer
Whose wet black muzzle nudges at destiny's gates—
It begs for lightness and laughter, for likemindedness,
For Lel, for pure *L,* a tired body
Longing to be lulled by harmony.
And its head is a dictionary
Of *L*-words only.
Like a polecat alone in an alien place, looking for
  love . . . poor cat!
Roistering *R,* sweep on,
Dulling the parquet's luster!
Subtract the area of the path from your barriers.
The murmur of folk lore
Becomes the roar of an angry nation;
The peasant's lumbering step
Becomes the rumble of revolt.
R, you are air, forced air, you make trains move
Like a chain-linked team of blood molecules

Through the veins of northern Siberia.
You power palaces across the waves;
Your force makes the highroads fork, they flourish like sun-
 flowers.
Then *L* began, and *R* declined and fell.
The nation drifts idly in a vessel of laziness:
The battering ram becomes a sacrificial lamb,
And the roar of the storm becomes a stale roll.
Those are now sold who once took up the sword,
Raw life becomes once more a life of law—
The serfowner possesses only his naked self.
But *R* ignites fires in dusty, abandoned files,
The saving wall is now rank with destroying war.
No longer lavishes, but only ravishes!
Routing light forever with the iron of its right,
Gallops its proud horse where the farmer has plowed
  To trample his field, to be everywhere feared,
To reduce the self again to serf.
R is a presence echoes twice in every prophet,
And turns poor players to their prayers.
It pierces the darkness of the days
When *K* resounded in Kolchak.
K has knotted a whiplash
Of shackles, decrees, kicks, commands, and rocks—
The prophets perished by means of these:
They all contain killing, and death at the stake.
When you, *R,* raised a howl
In the ears of these Northern calms,
The wide ears of these watery Northern calms:
"Take arms, brothers, take arms!"
A hunt by a hut, and a white hound
  On the heels of a thunderstorm,
And soldiers on the march once more,
  Till nothing is left but the last ha-ha
Of the skulls of the two last people
  On the platter of war.
That was the time when *K* moved over the steppe
With the heavy tread of a suicide,
Walking unsteadily toward *L* as a drunkard might walk,

Smearing his colors on the clouds of destiny,
Channeling a new course for the river of human deaths.
With the final hand of the ruined gambler,
Pistol at his forehead, *K* walks, very pale.
  R, Rah, Roh!
  Hark, the Dog-bark—
  God of Russia, god of Ruin!
Perun, your god, is giant-high—
He knows no bounds, he wrecks, he rends, he rips, he ruins.
Wrong to claim Kaledin is killed, and Kolchak,
  That a shot was heard.
That was the silence of *K,* that was *K* recoiling,
  K collapsing to the ground.
It is *L* who lulls the roar of terror, mends the riven tear—
  L, teller of the living tale.

First Passerby He's kind of clever.

Second Passerby But he hasn't got the true poetic fire. It's all just raw material, his sermon. Just a lot of unworked stuff. A lot of green wood. Go dry out, thinker . . .

PLANE EIGHT

Zangezi *R, K, L, G*—
Alphabet war-makers—
They were the actors in the drama of those years,
Warrior-heros of those days.
The will of nations surrounded their forces,
As wet water falls from the oars.
He looks for a lifeboat, a leg up, a lift,
a limb—who looks? Who falls into water,
into a crevasse, an abyss, a ravine.
A drowned man sits in the boat; he pulls on an oar.
It's a broad-bottomed boat, it stays afloat,
And languorously slows to a standstill.
K in chains, in vain in chains,
While *G* and *R* collide in combat.

G falls, cut down by *R*,
And *R* now lies at the feet of *L!*
Let the all-seeing sounds of a universal language
Whirl away the mists of time.
That language is light.
Now listen:

A Song in "Star-Language"

Within a haze of green *KHA,* two figures,
The *EL* of their clothes as they move,
A *GO* of clouds above the games they play,
The *VE* of a crowd that circles an unseen fire,
The *LA* of labor and the *PE* of games and songs.
The *CHE* of the young man is his bright blue shirt;
The *ZO* of his shirt—its glow and its gleam.
The *VE* of curls around his face
The *VE* of branches on the pinetree trunk
The *VE* of stars, the night-world turning overhead.
A *CHE* of girls—golden shirts,
A *GO* of girls—garlands of wildflowers,
A *SO* of rays of happiness;
VE of people in a ring
With *ES* of springtime pleasure,
MO of sadness, grief, and sorrow.
And the *PI* of happy voices,
The *PE* of peals of laughter,
The *VE* of branches when the wind blows—
A brief *KA* of rest.
Maidens, men, more *PE*! More *PI*!
KA comes to us all in the grave!
ES of laughter, *DA* like a rope of hair,
And the groves—the *KHA* of springtime rituals,
The oak grove—*KHA* of the god's desires,
Eyebrows—*KHA* of springtime glances
And braids—*KHA* of midnight faces.
And *MO* of long curling hair,
And a *LA* of labor while all is in motion
And the *VE* of merrymaking, *PE* of happy talk
The *PA* of a white shirt sleeve,

The *VE* of dark braids in coils,
The *ZI* of eyes.
Golden *RO* of young man's hair.
PI of laughter! *PI* of horseshoes and the clink of sparks!
MO to torment and longing.
MO to yesterday's sorrow.
The *GO* of a rock high above them,
The *VE* of river waves, the *VE* of wind and trees,
GO—the night-world's constellation.
TA of a shadow in evening—a girl,
And a *ZA-ZA* of delights—her eyes.
The *VE* of people circling an unseen fire.
The *PE* of singing
And the *RO* of singing heard in silence,
The *PI* of voices, calling out.
That is what star-language is like.

Voices from the Crowd Not bad, thinker! You're getting better all the time!

Zangezi These are star-songs, where the algebra of words is muddled with yardsticks and clocks. And this is only a first draft! Someday this language will unite us all, and that day may come soon.

First Passerby He's a divine liar. He lies like a night full of nightingales. Look up there—those flyers flying overhead. What do they say? (*he reads the flyers as they pass overhead*):

"*V* means the revolution of one point around another (circular motion).

L is the cessation of fall, or motion generally by a plane lateral to a falling point.

R is a point that penetrates a transverse area.

P is the rapid movement of one point away from another, and hence of many points, a multitude of points, from a single point; the expansion of volume.

M is the dispersion of volume into infinitely smaller parts.

S is the movement of points out from one motionless point; radiation.

K is the encounter and hence the halt of many moving

points in one motionless point. Hence the ultimate meaning of *K* is rest, immobilization.

KH is a surface that serves to shield one point from another point moving toward it.

CH is a hollow volume whose void contains a different body. Hence a bent or curved shield.

Z is the reflection of a ray from a mirror. The angle of incidence is equal to the angle of reflection (vision).

G is the movement of a point at right angles to the fundamental line of movement, away from it. Hence height."

First Listener He's getting a little out of hand with these flyers of his, that Zangezi! What do you think of all this?

Second Listener He has me hooked. I'm a fish wriggling on the harpoon of his ideas.

Zangezi Have you heard me? Have you heard all I've said, heard my speech that frees you from the fetters of words? Speech is an edifice built out of blocks of space.

Particles of speech. Parts of movement. Words do not exist; there are only movements in space and their parts—points and areas.

You are now set free from your ancestral chains. The hammer of my voice has shattered them; your frenzied struggle against those chains has ended.

Planes, the lines defining an area, the impact of points, the godlike circle, the angle of incidence, the fascicule of rays proceeding from a point or penetrating it—these are the secret building blocks of language. Scrape the surface of language, and you will behold interstellar space and the skin that encloses it.

PLANE NINE: THOUGHT

Quiet! Quiet! He's about to speak!

Zangezi Sound the alarm, send the sound through the mind! Toll the big bell, the great tocsin of intelligence! All the inflections of the human brain will pass in review before you, all the permutations of *OOM!* Look up and see! Join us now, all of you, in song!

I. *GO-OOM*
OUR-OOM
OOW-OOM
FAR-OOM
WITH-OOM me
And those I don't know
OM-OOM
OB-OOM
DAL-OOM
CHE-OOM
BOM!
BIM!
BAM!

II. *PRO-OOM*
PRA-OOM
PREE-OOM
EXCL-OOM
DEV-OOM
OR-OOM
ZA-OOM
FREE-OOM
VAV-OOM
RE-OOM
BY-OOM
BOM!

Help me, bell ringers, I'm tired.

III. *DOD-OOM*
DAD-OOM
MEE-OOM
RAY-OOM
ECHO-OOM
KHA-OOM

Sound the alarm, send the sound through the mind! Here is the bell and here is the bellrope.

IV. *DULL-OOM*
FROM-OOM
IN-OOM

ON-OOM
DVOO-OOM
TRE-OOM
DE-OOM
BOM!
OZ-OOM
OK-OOM
WITH-OOM
OP-OOM
AGL-OOM
AR-OOM
NO-OOM
DAY-OOM
FREE-OOM
BOM!
BOM! BOM, BOM!

Toll the great tocsin of intelligence!
The divine sounds descending, summoned by the voice of mankind! Beautiful is the sound of the mind! Beautiful are its pure crystal sounds.
But look now! See where *M* appears, and enters the range of *ICAN*, the land of *MOG*, the hold of the strongword *MOGU*.
Now listen to the word, listen to the mogogospel, listen to the bell-pull of power.

[*What follows are Khlebnikov's notes to Plane Nine*]

FREE-OOM. This is figurative. Of course rejecting what is old leads to free-oom.

NO-OOM. The hostile mind, leading to different conclusions, the mind that says "no" to any proposition.

GO-OOM. The mind that towers like those celestial trinkets unseen by day, the stars. When rulers fall, it picks up their fallen staff *GO*.

LA-OOM. Of great breadth, covering the greatest possible area, without banks or bounds, like a river in flood time.

KO-OOM. Tranquil, binding, establishing foundations, books, rules and laws.

LA-OOM descends from the heights to speak to the masses. It describes to the plain what is visible from the mountaintop.

CHE-OOM raises the cup to an unknown future. Its dawns are chesightings. Its rays are cherays. Its flames are cheflames. Its will is chewill. Its sorrow is chesorrow. Its delights are chedelights.

OM-OOM. The disastrous, shattering, destroying mind. It is foretold within the bounds of faith.

DEV-OOM. The mind of discipleship and of true citizenship, of a spirit of devotion.

OUR-OOM. Abstract, observing everything around it, from the vantage point of a single thought.

FROM-OOM. A leap beyond the boundaries of the ordinary mind.

DA-OOM. Affirmative.

NO-OOM. Argumentative.

DULL-OOM. Half-wit.

WITH-OOM. Collaborative.

DAY-OOM. Commanding.

ECHO-OOM. The secret, hidden intelligence.

BY-OOM. Craving intelligence, called into being not by what is, but by what it desires.

EXCL-OOM. Negation.

PRO-OOM. Prevision, foresight.

PRA-OOM. The intellect of a distant land, the ancestor-mind.

RE-OOM. Heeding the voice of experience.

VAV-OOM. The nail of an idea, driven into the plank of stupidity.

FREE-OOM. Escaping from the bonds of stupidity.

RAR-OOM. Recognizing no limits or boundaries, a shining, radiant mind. Its speeches are rahorns.

ZO-OOM. The mind reflected.

PLANE TEN

Back, Bog! Move, Mog!
March, Manmuscle!
I am Maker, and might!
I am Mover, and may! I am Matter, and might!
I am the Mighty Mower! Moving, improving! Mow might, Michman!
Magnet-eyed magus! Moving! Improving!
Musclemarch!
March, Michman! Hands! Arms!
Mammering, mowering force-face, full of muchness!
Matchering eyes, michering thoughts, muchering brows!
See my face, my mighthead! My arms, my mighthood!
—My hands, my arms!
Might-maker, main-mantle, motor-matter,
Motivated power-mower! Mogre!
My force-face mamogrified!
Many-mastering, Mog-mating muscle,
You shake your hair like a mountain-mogre,
A manifold maze, a nest of moglings, of muchlets and mainlings,
Of mightlings and masterkins, muchable mightlemames,
Where one miggle madlet still writhes
In a mowering moggle of magistry, a mag of might,
A breeding herd of mightlings and muchlets.
The raven beats her wings, brings water in her beak.
I must hurry so I will not be late!

See my face, Manmuscle! Magus of magnitudes!
Master of muchness!
Mickle miches! Major motion picture!
I move like fire-power, mogeyman, monster of men's
magination.
Mickle miches in a little magoom.
Move, Manmuscle!
Mog's overmowering muchness! Mammering Mog!
Man's-marrow! Power-mirror!
Magnify, mind, my magnimind! Hands, magnify!
Arms, mogrify!
Mutcher, Michman, magic Mogasm!
Move!
Magus of magnitudes! Master of muchness!
Moogle-eyes! Mog-mouth!
Michness of muchnesses!

Now *M* has invaded the lands and the holdings of Bog, destroying the fear of Him, achieving our necessary victory. Now the infantry army of *M* has ground down the rock of the impossible impassible, the stone age savage! Ground it into meal, into minute particles, matter for mites. They reduce a tree to moss and meadowgrass, an eagle to a moth, an elephant to a mouse and a mosquito. The one whole becomes the many, a mass of minute elements.

Now is the coming of *M,* mallet that mauls the great; omnivorous moth to mange the fur coats of centuries.

Now let us wake the sleeping gods of speech.

Shake the bastards by the beard! Wake up, you old ones! I am the Mogogur, the guru who gospels the name of *M!* Might-maker of Might-makers! Our course lies toward *M,* humanity's North Star, our polar point, the pole that supports the haystacks of our beliefs. Toward *M* the barque of the centuries sails, toward *M* the dugout of humanity sails, a proud breath filling the sails of governments and states.

We have come from the land of the mind to the mighty domain of *MOG.*

A Thousand Voices (muffled) *MOG! (pause) MOG! (pause) MOG!*
We are here! We are we!

The Distant Mountains *MOGOOOO! MOGOOOO!*

Zangezi Listen, the mountains acknowledge your declaration. Can you hear that proud flourish? "*MOGOOOO,*" the mountains reply to your claim of possession! A thousand voices repeat it in the clamoring canyons! Can you hear the gods beating their wings, startled up by our shouting?

The Crowd The gods are flying away! The gods are flying away!

PLANE ELEVEN

(The gods fly beneath the clouds; the air is filled with the beating of their wings.)

The Gods Hahahá ha hehheh héh!
Graka hata grororó
Leelee éghee, lyap, lyap, bém.
Leebeebeébee neeraró
Seenoáhno tseetseereéts.
Heeyu hmapa, heer zen, chénch
Zhoóree keéka seen sonégha
Hahoteeree ess esséh
Yunchee, enchee, ook!
Yunchee, enchee, peepoká.
Klyam! Klyam! Eps!

Voices in the Crowd The power of our voices has terrified the gods! Is that good? Is that bad?

PLANE TWELVE

Zangezi Ah! Now Alphabet advances!
Now is the danger time! The roofbeams of *M*
Begin to reach above the clouds.
Now hear the heavy step of *K*.
Again the spears of *G* and *R*
Impale the corpses of clouds,
Both fall dead, and then begins

The rivalry of *L* and *K*—
Their negative doubles.

R looks into the mirror of minus one and sees *K; G* looks and sees *L*. Higher than the anthill of human hopes, the great foundation pile of battles crams the sky with its blocks and columns, like one enormous war built up out of pilings and beam angles.

But the wind has scattered it all.

The power of our voices has terrified the gods.

Have you ever seen *L* and *K,* and the clash of their swords? And the fist of *K,* a handful of foundation piles, stretching out toward the austere columns of the armor of *L?*

Ah, Kolchak, Kaledin, Kornilov—are they only cobwebs, traces of mildew still left on that fist? Who are these fighters locked in a struggle beyond the storm clouds? A free-for-all, the battle of *G* and *R, L* and *K!* Some have grown hoarse, three are corpses, *L* is alone. Silence.

PLANE THIRTEEN

Zangezi They are the bright blue stilland,
The sky full of bright blue eye-fall,
Never-never fleeing things
Whispering on irrelevant wings.
Ledglings in flight, seeking their selfland,
Flocking through darkness to vanishment.
A swelling of heavenly neverings,
A swirling of wing-welling overings.
They have flown, fading and groaning,
Forgetting their getting, their names,
Unwillingly lulled in their own unwantings.
Cryers and callers, all whirled into wasteland,
Earth's own backward, the everlasting everlost of heaven,
Into the goneness of here and the notness of now,
Hovering haveless through star-frost and sea-spray
Toward elsewhere. Wayfarers on the evening air,
Thistening like thought-secrets, heaven's harriers,
These nestlings of nowhere, a lattering flutter

Of wings in flight to some elsewhere,
Of ledglings in flight, seeking their selfland!
Hover-home, breeder of streaming light,
Of strange unattainable flutter and fluxion!
Wing-wavers white as drifting down,
Weary wizards of downward drift
Wavering dowsers of dawn
River of blue skystead
Weary wings of the dreamstead
Broad harmonies of the downstead
Barefooted in star clusters
There you died.
Heaven hovers in their hair
Heaven hovers in their voices
Streaking the eastern stream of everland
They fly away into their neverland.
With the nevering eyes of earthlings
Like notnesses of earth-law.
Fleet flight to the blue of heaven,
Flight fleet into blue, hovering.
Shrouded in all-knowing sorrow
They fly to the source of pre-knowledge,
Winglings of no-where, mouths of now-here!
Winglings of not-here, mouths of no-there!
Heaven hovers in their faces:
They are the dwellers in the blue places,
High heaven's harriers, a flood of flame,
The heavenly fire-river over us all.
Their untamed eyes all vanishing vision,
Their untamed mouths saying: not-here.

Disciples Zangezi! We want something more down to earth! We've had enough of this sky stuff! Play us a tune we can dance to! You're supposed to be a thinker, think us up some entertainment. Everybody here wants to be entertained. That's the way things are—we just had a good dinner and we want to relax!

PLANE FOURTEEN

Zangezi Listen to me, you
Fair higherns of the gray mountains,
You hurry, you flurry of water descending,
Stormfall of waterflow over the cliff face,
Gray tusks of waves.
And you graylings of clouds,
Neverings of thunderheads hovering
Over a whirl-wave of grass.
And the whorl-wave too of the gray current
In the wide-spreading grayfulness of water.
I am the God-Maker, Divificator,
Walker of edges, and here I stand
Like a stack.

Now the black mammoth of the almost-dark,
A spill, an upset inkwell splashing
The milk of the ravine,
Raises his tusks of white water
Threatening these leaves of divine grass,
The orchard-grass, as his foot pilings
Trample the gooseweed
Making the grasses groan: God, oh God!
Threatening, then toppling into the abyss.
Wind-song and wing-sound from the wild steppe,
Night's dark blue river of lull and loll,
And springtime's nightly goodling freshens the higherns of grasses
In the wind's amble, on the fire-shoals of the sky!
Come younglings! Come lordlings!
The will-wave lapses and the wind's sweet sirring subsides.
Fate-flow of fatality, whirl-waves of divinity, receding in ripples.
And I am the God-Maker, Divificator,
Left all alone.

Voices From the Crowd What a mad muddle!
This is all a lot of gabble!

This is vain bibble-babble,
Zangezi! What language are you trying to talk?

Zangezi I go on!
You! It's you, you boot-eyed ladies,
Striding in shiny boots of night
Through the heaven of my poems!
Scatter the coins and tokens of your eyes
Over all the highways!
Draw the adder's coiling fang
From your hushabye hair.
Look through these cracks, through these fractures
of hatred.
I am the Fool-Maker, Duncificator, and here I sing
and rave!
Look at me jump up and down! Look at me dance
Here on the edge of a cliff!
When I sing, the stars applaud me
And I am worth every bit of it. Nothing can stand
Against me, here I stand. Stand!

Move ever onward, Planets of Earth!
Thus by plural number does my greatness cast its spell.
I am the Many-Maker, Multiplicator of Planet Earth:
Wobble yourself into hordes of earths,
Spin yourself, Earth, into swarms of mosquitos:
I sit alone, with folded arms,
Singer of the grave-ground.

I am what is not.

I am the only son of who I am.

PLANE FIFTEEN

(And now here are some soundwritten songs: the sounds are sometimes bright blue, sometimes dark blue, sometimes black and sometimes red.)

Soundwriting

VÉH-O-VEYA—the green of a tree
NEEZHEÓTY—the dark tree trunk
MAM-E-ÁMEE—that's the sky
PÓOCHE CHAPI—a blackbird
MAM EE EMO—that's a cloud

The odor of things is numerical.
Daylight in the garden!
And here is your holiday, your Labor Day.

LELI-LILI—the snow of locust flowers shielding a rifle
CHEÉCHECHÁCHA—the shine of sabers
NEE-EH-ÉNZAI—the scarlet of banners
ZEE-EH-ÉGZOI—the words of an oath
BÓBO-BEÉBA—the stripe of scarlet
MEEPEEÓPEE—the glitter of the gray-eyed troops
CHÚCHU BEÉZA—the glitter of swear words
MEE-VEH-ÁH-A—the heavens
MEEPEEÓPEE—the glitter of eyes
VE-E-ÁH-VA—the green of the troops!
MEEMOMÁYA—the dark blue of hussars
ZEEZOZÉYA—the sun's handwriting, a rye field of sun-eyed sabers
LELI-LÍLI—the snow of locust flowers
SOSESÁO—mountains of buildings·

The Listeners All right! That's enough! Please! Go suck a sour pickle, Zangezi! Give us something with substance! Something with some guts! Somebody light a fire under him! Look what kind of audience you've got! See? Even the rabbits have come out to listen! They sit there squinting and scratch their ears. Zangezi! Leave all this bunny business to the bunnies! Are we not men? Look how many of us have gathered here! Zangezi! You're putting us to sleep! That stuff sounds beautiful, but there's nothing to it! We want fire! We're cold! And this is lousy wood you've cut, it won't heat up our stoves!

PLANE SIXTEEN: THE FALLING SICKNESS

What's the matter with him? Somebody grab him!
One, two . . . Mount up! One, two! Ready, *mount!*
Ready . . .
Yeesh, you rat! Halt! Rarrh . . . Rarrh . . .
You White hoodlum! You'll never get away! You'll never
get away!
Halt, you bastard, stop it, calm down!
I'll slit your throat . . . Halt, you rat!
Halt, you rat! ARRGH!
grrr . . . grrr . . .
Rarrh!
Rarrh . . .
You'll never get away . . .
You lie . . . Halt!
Halt!
Rarrrh . . . Rarrrh . . .
grrr . . .
Hurrah . . .
ARRGH! ARRGH!
You lie, you bastard!
Sonofabitch!
Mother of God!
We don't spare heads
For freedom for Reds!
First Ossetian Cossack troop,
DRRRAW Sabers!
Forward! Follow me, men!
Right side cut,
Left side hack!
grrr . . . grrr . . .
You'll never get away!
Listen buddy,
Got a knife?
I'll cut his . . . Money bastard,
You lie! You'll never stop us now!
AIIEEEEEEE! Got you! You lie!
ARRGH! ARRGH!

Zangezi He's having a seizure. This is the falling sickness:
War-fear has wounded his soul.
War cuts our days like a throat.
This man has been seized—and he shows us
That war exists, that it still exists.

PLANE SEVENTEEN

Trio Well, we gotta get going.
Take it easy, Zangeezi.

(They start to go.)

There's an awful lot of traffic.
You've collected a crowd.
Let's go across the river and into the trees.
Hey, wait a minute, wait a minute. Where have
All the gods gone?
Yeah, who's gonna light my fire?
Yeah, who's got a light?
Who's got a cigarette?
I can't find the matches we used to use.
Come on, you guys, we can smoke on the way.
OK, so let's go.
Think we'll ever get together again?
Sure. We'll be best buddies in the sweet bye and bye.
Oh, I got a little bottle of homemade booze,
Gonna get God drunk, get rid of his blues.
So bring on the bimbos and let's have a party!
Yeah, let's get high! Roll your own!
Light up the sky! You get me my own and I'll roll her.
Yahoo!
Cockadoodle-do!
I'm gonna get to heaven and be right at home
From three to six every afternoon!
Onward, onward, only kids get scared,
We're big boys now . . . and ain't that too damn bad!
We'll do it our way, we'll drink the old way,
We'll drink the saints in heaven blind,
We'll drink to our Odessa-mama

And the moon of Alabama, and
We gotta dance! And drink some more!
Then we'll lie down and die like this Cossack on the floor.
Hey, Zangezi!
You on our side, Zangezi?
You got a match, Zangezi?

Zangezi Here, take these. These are the matches of Destiny.

Trio Yes*sir!*

(They go off.)

PLANE EIGHTEEN

Zangezi Nossir. The gathering storm is never an illusion.
Ardent, impassioned Ryleev
demanded death from the royal House of Rurik
(poison flows in the veins of every king)
and he dangled in the gallows-dance.
For Ryleev, Death was sweeter than chains.
The naked storm rushes above us.
The cause of freedom is afoot!
Let them lie quiet in their graves.
After two to the thirteenth—
the year was eighteen-forty-eight—
shepherds of hordes, red hordes.
The wind of freedom,
a day of universal storm!
The Poles rose up in revolt
disdaining the catcalls of destiny:
destiny's cheeks puffed out, her twisted mouth in a whistle;
the grim East frowned like the point of a gun, uncompromising,
harsh as the sound of gunfire, the point of a rifle,
frowned at the springtime of Poland's uprising.
But after three to the fifth, or two hundred forty-three
days have been scattered like coins of gold,
a sudden fiery shot, like the idea of death

on death row, a pistol bullet in the heart
of Berg, the insurgents' fatal full stop:
Pacifier of Poland, Viceroy of Poland,
rude precursor of the clank of chains.
See there—that chainlink glitters:
after three to the fifth, the moment of vengeance,
a shot, and the sight of gunsmoke, curling upward.
Consider the American president. Garfield elected!
The ice of distrust is broken.
Then, after three to the five, savagery stalks
and Garfield lies dying, lies dead.
Consider the streets of Rome,
the pillaging hordes from the East
who bound the white city in dark heavy chains,
provided a meal for legions of crows.
After two times three to the eleventh
a mountain of skulls grew out of
a battle, the field of Kulikovo—
Moscow has written a clean copy
of the rough draft of the first Rome's fate,
with the ink of its initial victories.
The machine-gun fire of the Eastern invasion grew silent.
One unforgettable battle, it cleaned out
the cartridge clip of the Eastern invasion.
The miller of time
has erected a skull-heap, a dam
from the bones of Kulikovo.
Across the steppe, the cry of "stop!"—
Moscow stands guard.
Hordes of nations galloped against the West,
wave after wave:
Goths and Huns, and then the Tatars.
After two times three to the eleventh
Moscow arose in her helmet of snowstorms
and cried to the East: not one step more!
The land grew sterile, it whitened beneath the Tatar yoke.
For a long time their inundation glittered.
Then Yermak with his daredevil laughter—
setting his stern brow at an angle,

testing the wind with his broad beard—
sailed the beautiful rivers of Siberia
to the far-off city of Kuchum.
The tenderest thing in the world
cannot stop him.
The die was cast and the victor's lot
shown in the water's reflection;
stars over Isker sparkled
and Moscow acquired one half of the world.
The snouts of bears sniffed at the oncoming Russians,
bear cubs tumbled at play on the rock piles,
the elk and its offspring migrated in hordes.
Enticing prizes, the pelts of sables
attracted the heavy boyars of the capital.
Voevodas set out to discover new lands,
they sailed through Northern oceans, through seas of ice.
When the Tatar Troubles were finally over,
it was Russia's turn to inherit the East.
And then two times three to the tenth
after the taking of Isker,
after the stern eyes of Yermak
reflected in Siberian rivers,
came the day of the battle of Mukden
when all that daring returned unto dust.
That is always the way: after three to the *n*th power,
comes the moment of shift, of reversal.
Yermak becomes Stessel
after three to the tenth days
and as much again.
What Kulikovo was for the Tatars
the horror of Mukden became for the Russians.
Like a prophet in eyeglasses
at his writing desk, Vladimir Solovyov
foresaw it all.
If Stessel loved piglets—
then he was Yermak after three to the tenth.
And Bulgaria, when she had
broken the chains of her overlord
and risen up free after so many years

by the vote of an international tribunal—
that valley of flowers—
it was because of the time that had passed,
three to the eleventh power,
from the day of the battle of Trnovo.
When Kiev was taken by Tatars
camels were stabled in the cathedrals,
the Russian capital was taken—
but three to the tenth power passed
and on the heights of Angora
Tamerlane met Bajazet.
Let Bajazet sit in his cage,
the Mongols themselves were rebuffed
after another power of three,
the dawn of their power shifting toward darkness.
Here, there, everywhere, the sword submits
to the ancient power of odd and even.
A watch tower is built of twos and threes
and the abbot of time paces its summit.
Where tattered military banners pecked the air
and horses are stubbornly silent,
only their echoing hoof resounds.
The Dead! The Living! Alike, all discarded!
These are the iron batons of time,
the axes of events, armature for the straw man of the universe.
The scarecrow of war is supported by rods
like the iron rods that frame up a strawman.
Number is the wire of the universe.
What are these? Barques of Truth?
Or empty stories?
The waves of the East and the West
alternate by a power of three.
The Greeks fought the Persians in gold-crested helmets,
from cliffs they hurled the invader harshly into the sea.
Marathon—and the defeated East
ebbed away, burning its ships behind it.
They pursued them and cut across the steppe.
After four times

three to the eleventh power—
Constantinople waits for the battle axes!
A tobacco spark ignites the temple-church,
everything falls to the Turks.
Your prince on his handsome horse
will be swallowed up in the flames.
The trader tosses his profits
overboard, for the Turks approach,
and disaster comes with them.
1917. The Tsar abdicates. The white mare of freedom!
A wild gallop, a breakthrough.
The two-headed eagle smashed in the square.
The mare's dark eyes glitter
with the image of a knife;
the grip of autocracy
can no longer rein her in.
She gallops, her hooves swirl up the dust,
galloping proud as a prophetess.
Behind her the dead past
breaks, it tears apart on the rocks.
Where is she galloping? What does she want?
You will never catch up!
All this dust makes it hard to keep up.
Fire and darkness burn in her eyes
and that is
because:
two to the twelfth power days
have passed
since the day of bloody Presnia.
Here the number two was the god of time
and the tsars fell, still clutching the bridle,
and the far-off halloo of distant pursuit
was a magic horn in the distance.
The voices of cannons
shook old Moscow's south embankment;
Minin's monument bowed its cast-iron curls
before the shells of Min descending everywhere.
It was a celebration of Min's birthday.
The laughter of guns from Sparrow Hills

stunned the most beautiful icons,
the Mothers of God of Moscow,
in the depths of their chapels.
It is Pushkin, who cuts the *n* from his name
like a lock of his curly hair—canonical Pushkin
becomes cannonical, blasting, pushing with the power
of a misplaced *n*.
Min was victorious.
He declaimed an *Onegin* of steel and lead
in the deaf ears of the crowd.
He intended to set himself up on the monument.
And after three to the fifth days
the snow turned bloody.
No one recognized him,
the crowds began to run,
and Min fell dead. Konopliannikova killed him.
After three to the fifth, two hundred and forty-three days
—precisely, more's the pity—
vengeance came,
that wonder of remorselessness:
steel pounded hard on humanity's bones,
the cannons stopped only on Sunday,
surrender seemed the only salvation.
The German sword above our heads
was an order to calamity and silence.
Then at last a peace treaty, a monkey on our back,
and after three to the fifth
an SR assassinated Mirbach.
If a knife is concealed in a fist
and revenge stares hard from the eyes,
then it's Time who howls: "I want!"—
and "Yessir," obedient Fate replies.

PLANE NINETEEN

(The people bring Zangezi a horse. He mounts.)

Zangezi Nickery, flickery,
Little stewball!
Coachery catchery,
Torturv morturv,
Matchery catchery, witchery watchery—
Evens in heavens
As evening descends,
Nickery, flickery,
Little stewball!
The storm is a seance
That I can see,
Signs of a science
The eye can see.
Hello, freedom,
Goodbye, force!
Giddyap, giddyap,
My good horse!

(He begins to ride toward the city.)

I have rivers for hair!
See where the Danube streams
Upon my shoulders!
Turbulent tantrums
Rip the Dnieper's blue rapids.
This is the Volga, the shining big-sea-water
And this long hair
That I twist in my fingers,
This is the Amur, where geishas gaze
Toward heaven, praying
Away the storm.
I am the master carpenter of time.
I have deciphered the timepiece of humanity,
And set its hands accurately,
Added a clockface, reckoned
The hours all over again,
Chiseled the lug nut into place.
The destiny hand of this steel heaven

Moves. I have faced it with crystal:
It ticks more quietly now, the way it used to.
I wear the timepiece of humanity
Casually, like a wristwatch.
The rachets and wheels of its works
Whisper their steel conversation.
I am a proud rider, a mender of brains.
They move and work the way they did before.
Clumps of intelligence, stacks of sense,
A wagon train of dead ideas,
Manure for God's eternal acres,
Their foreparts gods, and beasts behind,
Gather them like sheaves and stack them up with laughter,
Grant them several gaits, and make them swift and playful.
(These are things that furrow thinkers' foreheads,
These songs of the holy book.
Workers in the factory of thought!
Work, produce, deliver!)
Give them room to run, swiftness in maneuver,
And restlessness and fire.
Banish from their course
All conflict and disaster,
And let the stripling's curls
Fly the father's anger.
Marshal them on trains, on swift, night-moving steamships,
Let them eat the grass of stars
And follow humanity's highways
In deep galactic spaces.
Let the chill rush of every river
Entice them into open fields, persuade them to their rest.
And let the clip-clop of my cadences
Lie colt-like on the new-mown hay
And sleep like clumps of dreams
Worn out by springtime.
Planets of Earth! Forward, march!
Just suppose somebody throws
A net of numbers over the globe,
Does that mean he raises our minds?
No, it means our mind is more alone.
Once it meant slugs and snails—
Now it means living like eagles!
Rainbows growing every day!

Hooray!
Tomorrow the planet explodes
With a network of overhead roads!
Hooray!
And if somebody calls you a god,
You rant and rave and say:
It's a lie! God only comes up partway!
He's only as high as my heel!
Hooray!
We'll fly our existence away!
People are glaciers, about to flow!
The more we fly, the higher we go!
Everyone playing
To beat the band,
Batting the Planet
From hand to hand.
See the patterns of waves of sand
And the curly hair of the sea—
The beach, the branches, the debris.
Pinetree branches move a hand
And a book is written on the sand—
The book of the pine, the shore, the sea.
Sandy waves, a stand of pines
And someone nearby whistles,
I can hear their breath move in and out.
The sea by daylight
Chews on silence
Like a thrown-away bone.
Bluestorm sea beast, bluehair sea beast,
The slap, slap of its pelt on the shore.
A rock for a pillow,
A bush for a bed,
Sea foam for bedsheets,
And a swarm of stars for a comforter—
For that hermit from himself,
That dweller in the sea's fine mansions,
The ordinary wind.
I discontent you, Ocean:
You discontent me.
You pour out these mile-long stretches
Of speckled basket foam.
Pilings and pilings and pilings!

On a scaffold of pilings something menacing
Crouches, something ripened in secret
Like armfuls of dusky rye.
It's hard to make progress through waves of sand!
Who's there? It's the flower-seller sea.
Come down to the shore, sit next to me.
I'm an ordinary earthman, just like you!
Call me humanity. I am teaching
The suns of neighboring galaxies
To salute me—by the numbers—one, two!
Shouting at suns is a rough, uncompromising job.
I am a warrior; Time is a rifleman.
These are my leggings:
Rome in flames, charred and smoking,
A smouldering plank from her temples,
Laced up with equations
Stretched tight,
—That's legging number one.
And Constantinople, where a warrior
Perishes in flames,
—That's legging number two, and that works too.
You see I can stride
Back and forth
Across the centuries.
My leggings fit tight.
Room, friends, to roam!
I hear the call of great capital cities:
The great gods of sound
Shake the plates of Earth
And heap up the dust of humanity,
The dust of the family of man,
Humbled by each foundation stone,
Into huge capital cities,
Into lakes of standing waves,
Burial mounds of thronging thousands.
We breathe like a wind upon you,
We whistle, our breath moves,
We blow blizzards of nations,
We cause waves, we bring ripples and waves,
A measured groundswell moves
Across the smooth face of centuries!

We bring you war
And the downfall of empires.
We are the wild sounds!
We are wild wild horses,
Tame us.
We will carry you off
To other worlds,
Faithful to the wild
Rider
Of Sound.
Trumpet the charge, humanity!
Round up the herd of wild horses!
Saddle and bridle the Cavalry of Sound!

(Exit Zangezi.)

PLANE TWENTY: SORROW AND LAUGHTER

(The mountains are empty. A sudden goat leap, and Laughter appears on the platform, leading Sorrow by the hand. Laughter is a heavy man, hatless, wearing a white shirt and an earring in one ear. His black trousers have one leg blue, the other gold. He has jolly, fleshy eyes. Sorrow is dressed completely in white; only her hat is black. It has a broad low brim.)

Sorrow Call me Sorrow. I know the headstone of
Heartaches, as sadness knows a princess.
All my life is spent in longing—
Wind, come tear my braids to tatters!
I scratch my body with my nails,
I squeeze my head between my hands.
Yet swallows sing sweetly of places
Where longing no longer exists.
Sadness, universal sadness
Fills me, like a reservoir in floodtime.
I praise it with the curse of a woman
Deprived of a crust of bread.

Then why do you, eyes of the dead,
Seem awash with the wings of your need?
I flap like a fish in their fish trap,
A mermaid of otherworld seas.

Laughter Witloose in the hills of reason,
Chamois-light and sure of foot,
That's me. A happy heavy person.
I believe in all the me there is.
I wend my way like a walrus,
Lurching, making my dark flip-flop.
My laughter blossoms like the bright
Steel rainbow of a knife.
My laughter blossoms like the cruel
Steel passion of a knife.
I put my hard hands on my hips
And rattle the floor with my horseshoes.
Hear my single earring jingle.
With the logs of laughter's woodpiles
I stoke up my sky-blue brain.
With a wild ha-ha I let you know
That there's someone hiding behind this curtain,
I loosen the pinching shoes of reason
And hold out the old glad hand.
You raise your arms like drain pipes
Toward heaven's eyes,
And suck the rain of nighttime skies.
But I'm not like you; I'm crazy.
I'm a devil with fat-filled eyes.
Burn up like the fires of heathen temples,
Burn like candles in chapels of sadness!
Feel the laugh-fat here, on the back of my neck—
Your arms have embraced it,
Your kisses have tasted it.
I am the attic of a well-built roof,
Dry whatever the weather.
And you—you always see the deathsman, about
To cut away your soul with knives.
I am the attic of a pointed roof,
Dry in heavy showers of tears;
And you—you always see the deathsman, about
To fix your fatal midnight drink;

You are tied to a wheel like a saint;
The torture chamber breaks you.
You fence yourself off from the fun-fair
As a comma sequesters a phrase.
I draw out the curve of a smile
As we stand here together;
You twist on the cobweb of pain
While I hand you a flower.
We are two mistakes—one large, one small—
In the meadows of a nighttime smile.
I am Laughter, lightning rod
For universal anger.
You are a starry reservoir, our lady
Of universal sadness.
You always make me laugh at fate:
The more you cry,
The brighter in the sky
Shines the universal finger
That fate seems always so fond of.
You, you always make me laugh
At everyone who groans and suffers
And all you ever get is the finger
Of heaven, like a holy joke.
Your soul is a heavy carpet
Where the feet of the stars feel at home;
Yesterday I snitched away from heaven
A collection of cheap jokes.
You embrace the knees of universal sorrow
And you weep, while I start fights,
I fuss and argue, play the wise-ass,
And it ain't easy. Even a clown
Has his work cut out for him.
But people always look away
From your otherworldly eyes.
And if I get greasepaint in my mouth,
That doesn't mean I like the taste.
And still you let me keep
Your quiet kisses. You bring me love.
You are drawn to me forever,
I am a healing presence in your land.
Like stalks of wheat in summer fields
You bend beneath your tender guilty burden,

And I laugh my greasy laugh,
Laugh at my face and laugh at my fate,
When all in one moment you become my darling,
My obedient servant to command.

An Old Man These brand new rubles for the latter day
Are slick—but the eye of God sees through 'em.
I'll put 'em in the pockets of my nighttime pants.
Just like the taxman's jingling coffin.
Two hills in time are farther apart
Than your eyes and the back of your head.
I talk all wrong, I talk awry
And these graves never knew any better.
Precision's watchdog, I bring
Bookkeeping systems to swear words.
There's Fortune's fools, and there's those
Who live high off the hog—
Proud men and gun-men,
Prophets and con-men.
It's all one game of leap, frog:
It's the number game, with cut-off dates
In time. See my scissors? Hear their sinister click?
Watch, I'll cut his breath with deadly nightshade
And prune the wild babble of Laughter.
I move among humans, passing out shares
In graveyards. I send them funeral wreaths of envy.
And the man who sweats on his deathbed
Cannot take his eyes from mine.
So carry on, Laughter! And Sorrow,
Continue, that's my good mouse!
While I put on skull and white armor
And hang like a bogeyman over the house.
I'll shake the dry bones of my arm
Like a death rattle right in your face!
Oh, if only the curtain would rise
Again, only once, in the distance.
And those that drown in Kitezh-town
Will sleep in the dark beneath Sorrow's eyelids.
Run, children, run!
What happens in life we dare not dream.

Laughter I'm Laughter, I'm a lightning rod

Wherever thunder threatens.
Sorrow, you're the reservoir
Into which all ancient waters flow.
And the thunderstorm flies to its finish
Like the arrogant course of the corsair.
I have always seen the truth
In Sorrow's eyes, even drowned in mire.
I am the word's wild highwayman—
My words are the terror of the Volga!
But the faucets of your sadness
Wash my hands in good behavior.

Sorrow Subtle gloom of evening!
I feel the souls of hundreds here inside me.
I am uncanny, and that makes you sad.
Nets of tears tangle my eyelashes.
I dance like Kshesinskaia before the grave;
I sit here wordless, locked in thought,
Like Pototska in the castle of Girei.
But I was a child once and loved sweet things,
And delicate finches, those happy birds!
They please the eye of the passerby.
Bringers of berry-throated springtime,
Like dark red flowers
Budding on winter's wet, black bough.
But it's no use. Life is a desert, and you
Can never fill this hollow up with life,
Or tear the headstone from your grave.
One thing alone I see, always: the skull
That grins beneath your grinning face;
The hopeful, hankering worm that waits
To make his dinner on your muscular thigh.
My eye always brims
With black tears,
As a blue butterfly winks
On a black stone.

Laughter What if our wills and our tongues
And talk were one! Why not?
When Laughter finally leaves,
Everyone grieves!
A do-nothing day, an indolent hour!

You are flint, and I am fire!
But I must take old Laughter to the marketplace.
Now, you happy crowd of spectators,
You are about to witness in single combat
The duel of the swordblade and the skull.
Off with these clothes! Off with this shirt!
The tortoise takes to the skull road, the race has begun!
Tear this shirt, bare my shoulder—
That steel hairline held in a hand
Threatens me like a swordblade, a wordblade,
A voice from an ancient burial mound.
Move your braid the way it always moves
Like waves of rich black earth.
Its curve is a crescent moon of copper
Aimed at my heart.
The shirt billows broad and wide
And my muscles move freely;
It is time for the homespun of serfdom
To stop its eternal complaining.
Like a born fighter, I blaze bold
And hassle your sword from its scabbard.
Cling upon clang, like the scream of a wren
It cleaves the fish scale clean.
Time the skull-man, odd and even!
Now these iron lightning bolts
Suddenly bend and begin to oppose me!
Strait is the gate, and the path above the abyss!
Upon the snowfield of your shirtfront
A scarlet hedgerose starts to grow.
I am the marker of my own full stop.
We are all the perpetrators of our lives!
Begin then, begin! Slash away!
What we count is what counts, not what we say!
Remember the lightfoot month of May!
The choice we make will win the day!
Let fist hold fast
In the guard of a sword,
In the heavy mesh of metal chain.
A hundred biting bees attack
And an accurate riposte beats them back—
No one can even count their number.

Wilder and higher,
Like sparks from a fire,
Like flames from a pyre!
The movement of Time undoes us all.
Oh, what a fall!

(Laughter falls dead, clutching the red foam on his side.)

EPILOGUE: A CHEERFUL LOCATION

(Two people reading a newspaper.)

What's this? Zangezi is dead!
Not only that, but he did it himself, with a razor!
What terrible news!
What a sad story!
All he left was a little note that said:
"Razor, cut my throat!"
A lotus flower of shining steel, opening its petals,
Pushing through the water of his life
And now he's dead.
The motive seems to have been the destruction
Of all his manuscripts by fiendish
Villains with big broad chins
And lips that went smack smack, chomp chomp.

(Zangezi enters.)

Zangezi Zangezi lives!
It was all just a stupid joke!

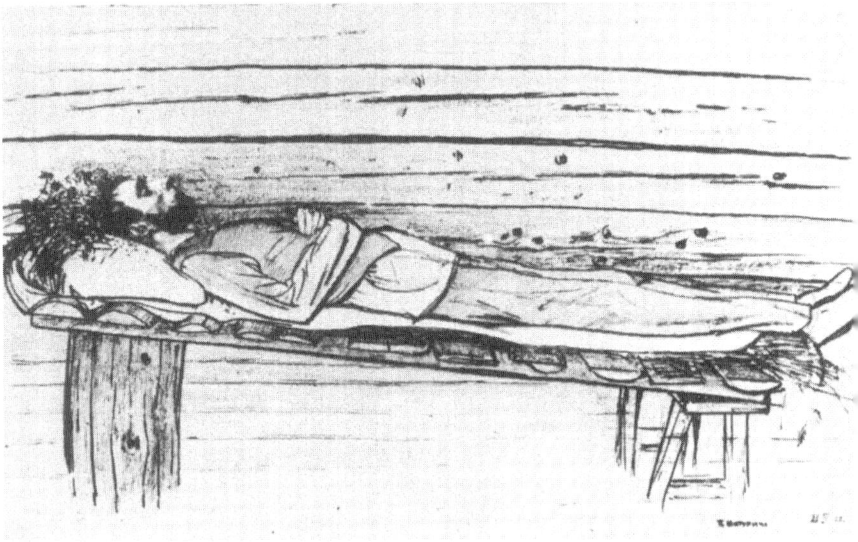

Pyotr Miturich, Khlebnikov on his bier, 1922

Chronology
Indexes

Chronology

	HISTORY	ARTS/SCIENCE	KHLEBNIKOV
1885			
	Marx's *Kapital*, vol. 2 (posthumous)	Ezra Pound born 1st automobile powered by internal combustion engine	November 9: K. born in village of Malye Derbety, ca. 50 miles south of Volgograd
1903			
	Split between Mensheviks and Bolsheviks at London congress Strikes in southern Russia	Wright brothers' first air flight	Graduates from Kazan gymnasium; enters university
1905			
	Bloody Sunday: police fire on demonstrators in St. Petersburg Japan defeats Russia in battles of Mukden and Tsushima Straits General strike and popular revolt in Russia Moscow uprising put down by Min	Einstein publishes Special Theory of Relativity	

	HISTORY	ARTS/SCIENCE	KHLEBNIKOV
1908		Rimsky-Korsakov dies	Sends early poems to Ivanov
	Bosnia and Herzegovina occupied by Austria with Russia's complicity		
		First Cubist paintings	Moves to Petersburg; enters university
		Minkowski publishes equations for four-dimensional manifold that links time and space	
1909			
	Tension between Russia and Austria over annexation of Bosnia and Herzegovina		Meets Kamensky
			Publishes first literary piece
		Marinetti's first Futurist manifesto published	
		Ostwald receives Nobel Prize for chemistry, Marconi for physics	
1910	Montenegro proclaimed a kingdom		Plans trip to Montenegro

	HISTORY	ARTS/SCIENCE	KHLEBNIKOV
1910 (continued)		Manifesto of Italian Futurist painters	Meets Burliuk and Matiushin
			Breaks with Ivanov and Symbolists
			"Incantation by Laughter" published in Kulbin's *Impressionists' Studio*
			The collection *A Jam for Judges* published; includes "O Garden of Animals!"
		Tolstoy dies	
1911		Kamensky's plane crashes in Poland	Meets Mayakovsky
	Russian prime minister Stolypin assassinated		Working on theory of history
		Tatlin production of *Tsar Maximilian* in Moscow	
		Matisse visits Russia	
		Scriabin publishes *Prometheus* (in Germany)	
		Kandinsky's "Concerning the Spiritual in Art" read at art congress in Petersburg	

	HISTORY	ARTS/SCIENCE	KHLEBNIKOV
1912	Bolshviks elect central committee	Hess discovers cosmic radiation	
	Titanic sinks		
	Bolsheviks edit *Pravda*		Visits Burliuk estate in southern Russia
			A Game in Hell by K. and Kruchonykh
		Du Cubisme by Gleizes and Metzinger	
	Wilson elected U.S. president		Contributes to *A Slap in the Face of Public Taste*
			The World in Reverse by K. and Kruchonykh
1913		Balashov slashes historical painting by Repin; Cubo-Futurists blamed	
	300th anniversary of the Romanovs		Contributes to *A Jam for Judges* II
	Balkan wars	Armory Show in New York	*Mrs. Laneen*
		Tatlin visits Picasso	"Usa-Gali"
			"Nikolai"
		Stravinsky's *Sacre du printemps* ballet in Paris	"The Word as Such"
			"The Letter as Such"
		Victory over the Sun, Cubo-Futurist opera	

	HISTORY	ARTS/SCIENCE	KHLEBNIKOV
1914		Marinetti visits Moscow, Petersburg	Breaks with Burliuk over Marinetti
		James Joyce's *Portrait of the Artist*	*Selections of Poems*
	World War I begins	First Tatlin abstract reliefs	*Creations*
1915	British-German naval battle of Dogger Bank		Writes "K" (pub. 1916)
		Filonov publishes *Prophesalvos of a Branching Universe*	
		Eliot's "Lovesong of J. Alfred Prufrock" published	
		Einstein presents General Theory of Relativity to Prussian Academy	
	Russia loses Poland, Lithuania, Courland	Scriabin dies	
		Malevich shows first Suprematist paintings	
1916		Franz Marc dies	Society of 317 (Presidents of Planet Earth) founded
	British-German naval battle of Jutland		Drafted into army
	Rasputin murdered		Stationed near Saratov

	HISTORY	ARTS/SCIENCE	KHLEBNIKOV
1917	February revolution; tsar abdicates		Receives military furlough
	Provisional government formed		In Kharkov, writes "An Appeal by the Presidents of Planet Earth"
	U.S. declares war on Germany	Satie and Picasso ballet *Parade*	
	October revolution; Lenin becomes head of new government		In Moscow and Petrograd; with Tatlin plans program of 3 plays
	Russian-German armistice		
1918	Civil war in Russia		
	Soviet Union adopts western calendar		
	Allied embassies leave Soviet Union	Malevich paints "White Square on White Ground"	
	Russian-German treaty of Brest-Litovsk	Blok's "The Twelve" published	
	New government moves from Petrograd to Moscow	Lenin abolishes Academy of Art	
	American troops land in Vladivostok		Works for newspapers in Nizhni-Novgorod

	HISTORY	ARTS/SCIENCE	KHLEBNIKOV
1918 (continued)		Classes start at Free Art Studios	
		Kandinsky active in visual arts section of Commissariat of Enlightenment	Works for newspaper in Astrakhan; writes "October on the Neva"
	Revolution in Germany; William II abdicates		
	Allied-German armistice		
1919		Abstraction and Suprematism exhibition in Moscow	
		First museum of modern art (Museum of Artistic Culture) organized in Petrograd	
	Third International founded in Moscow	Gropius founds Bauhaus at Weimar	
			Spends early spring in Moscow; contributes "The Head of the Universe" and "To the Artists of the World" to proposed collection, *International of the Arts*
		State Publishing House established	In military hospital with typhus
		Malevich moves to Vitebsk art school; publishes "On the New Systems in Art"	

	HISTORY	ARTS/SCIENCE	KHLEBNIKOV
1919 (continued)			
	Kolchak defeated by Bolsheviks in Urals	Einstein's General Theory confirmed	
1920			
	Prohibition begins in U.S.		In Kharkov, after release from hospital
	Allies withdraw from Siberia		
	League of Nations founded in Paris		
		Institute of Artistic Culture founded in Moscow; headed by Kandinsky	
		H. G. Wells visits Russia, received by Lenin	
			Arrives in Baku; works for newspaper and cultural-educational section of Volga-Caspian fleet
	Allies withdraw from southern Russia		In Baku invents Laws of Time
	Famine in Russia	Malevich publishes *Suprematism: 34 Drawings*	
1921			
	Famine in Russia		
	End of civil war		
	Rebellion at Kronstadt naval base put down by Red Army		

	HISTORY	ARTS/SCIENCE	KHLEBNIKOV
1921 (continued)			
	Lenin initiates New Economic Policy		Sails from Baku to Enzeli, Persia
		Blok dies	
		Gumilev shot	Returns to Russia; goes to Piatigorsk
		Isadora Duncan performs at Bolshoi in Moscow for 4th anniversary of revolution	Returns to Moscow
		Kandinsky leaves Russia	
		Einstein wins Nobel Prize for physics	
1922			Finishes *Zangezi*
		Joyce's *Ulysses* published in Paris	
	Lenin suffers first stroke		*Excerpt from the Tables of Destiny* published
		First continuous-wave transmissions from Shukov radio tower in Moscow	
	Union of Soviet Socialist Republics proclaimed		*Zangezi* printed
			June 28: K. dies in village of Santalovo
		Eliot's "The Waste Land" published	

INDEXES

The following indexes list all the titles and first lines of poems included in this book, first in Russian, then in English. Each entry is followed by the appropriate reference (in parentheses) to the Russian texts, abbreviated as follows:

Roman and arabic numbers—volumes and pages of Velimir Xlebnikov, *Sobranie proizvedenij* (Collected Works), ed. N. Stepanov and Ju. Tynjanov, 5 vols. (Leningrad: Izdatel'stvo pisatelej, 1928–1933)

NP—*Neizdanie proizvedenija* (Unpublished Works), ed. N. Xardžiev (Moscow: Xudožestvennaja literatura, 1940)

M.III—volume 3 of *Sobranie sočinenij* (Collected Works), ed. Vladimir Markov (Munich: Wilhelm Fink Verlag, 1968–1972), in the Slavische Propyläen series (no. 38, vols. 1–4), a republication of the Stepanov and Xardžiev editions with additional material, bibliography, and notes

Vroon—Ronald Vroon, *Velimir Xlebnikov's Shorter Poems: A Key to the Coinages* (Ann Arbor: University of Michigan, 1983), in the series Michigan Slavic Materials, no. 22

CGALI—Central State Archive of Literature and Art, Moscow

Parnis—a corrected and annotated version of the essay "Oktjabr' na Neve," published in *Literaturnoe obozrenie,* no. 2, 1980

Note: For those who are able to read Khlebnikov in Russian, it should be noted that there are variations between the texts we followed and the printed Russian editions in the cases of these titles: "!Futurian!," "The Solitary Player," "The lice had blind faith," "Russia, I give you my divine white brain," "OK, Graylegs," *Zangezi,* and *Excerpt from the Tables of Destiny.* In these instances we have relied on more accurate versions provided by Ronald Vroon, based on his review of the original manuscripts housed in the Khlebnikov archive in Moscow. His corrections will be published in detail in our forthcoming edition of the Collected Works.

Russian Index

"A rjadom v izbe s tesovoju kryšeju" (V.77) 47

Bex: Basnja (II.243) 23
!Budetljanskij! (V.193) 123
Bukva, kak takovaja (V.248) 121

"Vesennego Korana" (III.30) 25
"Vesny poslovicsy" (III.31) 25
"Veter—penie" (II.258) 29
"Vnimatel'no čitaju vesennie mysli" (V.66) 54
"Vozzvanie predsedatelej zemnogo šara" (V.162) 130
"Vremeši-kamyši" (II.275) 16
"V tot god, kogda devuški" (V.72) 52
"V uglu gromadnye materi temnejut glaza" (V.79) 48
"Vši tupo molilisja mne" (V.72) 52

"Gau! Gau! Gau!" (V.73) 51
"Gody, ljudi i narody" (III.7) 28
Golova vselennoj (CGALI, f.665, op. 1, ed. xr. 32, 1. 41) 144
"Golod gnal čelovečestvo" (V.81) 50
Gospoža Lenin (IV.246) 63

"Delo vaše, bogi" (V.66) 36
"Detusja! Esli ustali glaza byt' širokimi" (III.149) 37
"Dikij xoron" (Vroon, 210) 16
Doski sudby, otryvok (M.III.467) 169

Edinaja kniga (V.24) 41
"Esli ja obrašču čelovečestvo v časy" (III.295) 55
"Ešče raz, ešče raz" (III.314) 37

"Žarexu iz seryx myšej" (V.77) 47
"Žri že, ščenok" (V.80) 49

Zakljatie smexom (II.35) 20
"Zakon kačelej velit" (II.94) 28
Zangezi (III.315) 191
"Zelenyj lešij, bux lesinyj" (II.92) 21

Iranskaja pesnja (III.130) 44

K (IV.47) 85
"Kogda roga olenja podymajutsja" (II.95) 33
"Kogda umirajut koni—dyšat" (II.97) 28
"Komu skazaten'ki" (II.39) 21
"Korova byla" (V.78) 46
"Korol' v temnice" (NP, 410) 33
"Krylyškuja zolotopis'mom" (II.37) 24
"Kuril'ščik širy" (V.34) 43

"Ljudi, kogda oni ljubjat" (II.45) 30
"Ljutikov želtyx pučok" (NP, 167) 26

"Mal'čik na rečke dostal" (V.78) 46
Mirskonca (IV.239) 68

"Mne vidny—Rak, Oven" (II.30) 31
"Moj belyj božestvennyj mozg" (V.72) 53
My i doma (IV.275) 133
"My čaruemsja i čuraemsja" (II.42) 20

"Negol' sladko nežnoj skazki" (NP, 103) 15
Nikolaj (IV.40) 79
"Ni xrupkie teni Japonii" (II.205) 30
Noč' v Persii (V 36) 42
"Noči zapax—èti zvezdy" (V.83) 40
"Nu, taščisja, Sivka" (III.298) 56

"O, Azija! Sebja toboju muču" (V.32) 40
Odinokij licedej (III.307) 54
"O, Dostoevskij—mo" (II.89) 30
Oktjabr' na Neve (Parnis, 110) 105
"O sad! Sad!" (NP, 356) 17
O stixax (V.225) 152
Otkaz (III.297) 34
Otryvok iz dosok sud'by (M.III.467) 169
Oxotnik Usa-gali (IV.37) 76

Pa-ljudi (II.99) 35
Pesn' smuščennogo (NP, 157) 29
"Podan obed, pervoe bljudo" (V.78) 48
"Po ovragu lesnomu pyl' podymaja" (V.80) 50
"Pust' na mogil'noj plite pročtut" (NP, 318) 116
"Pust' paxar', pokidaja boronu" (NP, 195) 55

Radio buduščego (IV.290) 155

"Segodnja Mašuk kak borzaja" (III.187) 51
"Segodnja snova ja pojdu" (NP, 160) 34
"Segodnja strogoju bojarynej Borisa Godunova" (II.238) 36
"S žurčaniem-svistom" (II.41) 15
"S krotkim licom svečki sgorevšej" (V.79) 49
Slovo, kak takovoe (V.247) 119
"Slony bilis' bivnjami tak" (V.12) 24
"Snegič uzyvnyj, belyj i dlinnyj" (NP, 111) 16
"Studa besstydnyx neg" (NP, 108) 15
"Sutkonogix tabun kobylic" (NP, 119) 58
"Synoveet nôcej sineva" (III.104) 31

"Tam, gde žili sviristeli" (II.276) 16
"Tebja poju, moj sinij son" (II.277) 17
"Točit derev'ja i tixo tečet" (III.106) 29
Truba Marsian (V.151) 126
Truščoby (II.34) 22

"Usad'ba noč'ju, Čingisxan!" (II.217) 31
Utes iz buduščego (IV.296) 160

Xudožniki mira (V.216) 146

"Černyj car' pljasal pered narodom" (II.214) 24
Čisla (II.98) 28
"Čudovišče, žilec veršin" (II.40) 21

"Ja videl, babr sidel u rošči" (III.46) 21
"Ja vyšel junošej odin" (III.306) 33
Ja i Rossija (III.304) 35
"Ja slavlju let ego nasilij" (NP, 120) 15

English Index

"Alive with glad tidings" (III.30) 25
An Appeal by the Presidents of Planet Earth (V.162) 130
"Asia, I have made you my obsession" (V.32) 40
"Attentively I read the springtime thoughts of the Divinity" (V.66) 54

"Babylove, don't your eyes ever get tired" (III.149) 37
"Black king dance out front of the crowd" (II.214) 24
"Bow! Wow! Wow! (V.73) 51
"A boy down by the creek" (V.78) 46
"A bunch of yellow buttercups" (NP, 167) 26

"Came a rush of whistling" (II.41) 15
A Cliff Out of the Future (IV.296) 160
"Crawling crying craven" (Vroon, 210) 16

"Dinner is served, and here's the first course" (V.78) 48
"Dostoeskimo snowstorms" (II.89) 30
The Dregs of Opium (V.34) 43
"Dust in the air near the ravine" (V.80) 50

"Eat it up, puppy" (V.80) 49
"Enormous arboreal monster, horrid" (II.40) 21
Excerpt from the Tables of Destiny (M.III.467) 169

"The fault is yours, you gods" (V.66) 36
"The freezing weather of debauchery" (NP, 108) 15
!Futurian! (V.193) 123

"Genghiskhan me, you midnight plantation" (II.217) 31
"Glitter-letter wing-winker" (II.37) 24
"A greeny goblin grabbles in the forest" (II.92) 21

The Head of the Universe. Time in Space. (CGALI, f.665, op.1, ed. xr.32, 1.41) 144
"A herd of horses shod with Hours" (NP, 119) 58
"Here I praise the brutal flight" (NP, 120) 15
"Hunger herded humanity" (V.81) 50

"I'm going out again today" (NP, 160) 34
Incantation by Laughter (II.35) 20
"In the corner, mother's enormous eyes" (V.79) 48

"In the hut next door with the board roof" (V.77) 47
Iranian Song (III.130) 44
"I saw a Tiger, he crouched by a wood" (III.46) 21
"I see them—Crab, Ram, Bull" (II.30) 31
"It has the unassuming face of a burnt-out candle" (V.79) 49

K (IV.47) 85
"The King is out of luck" (NP, 410) 33

"Languor-wing lying in the middle of fable" (NP, 103) 15
"The law of the see-saw argues" (II.94) 28
The Letter as Such (V.248) 121
"Let them read on my gravestone" (NP, 318) 116
"Let the plowman leave his furrow" (NP, 195) 55
"The lice had blind faith, and they prayed to me" (V.72) 52

Mrs. Laneen (IV.246) 63

"The naked stag-horn rising in the woods" (II.95) 33
"Nations, faces, ages pass" (III.7) 28
Night in Persia (V.36) 42
"Night's color breeding darker blues" (III.104) 31
Nikolai (IV.40) 79
Numbers (II.98) 28

October on the Neva (Parnis, 110) 105
"O Garden of Animals!" (NP, 356) 17
"OK, Graylegs" (III.298) 56
"Once more, once more" (III.314) 38
The One, the Only Book (V.24) 41
On Poetry (V.225) 152
Ourselves and Our Buildings (IV.275) 133

"People in love" (II.45) 30
Po People (II.99) 35

The Radio of the Future (IV.290) 155
Refusal (III.297) 34
"Roast mouse" (V.77) 47
Rue: A Fable (II.243) 23
Russia and Me (III.304) 35
"Russia, I give you" (V.72) 53
"Rutting elephants, battering ivory tusks" (V.12) 24

"The sayings and sallies of spring" (III.31) 25
"The smell of night, and stars" (V.83) 40
"Snowfellow, tallfellow, bright beacon" (NP, 111) 16
The Solitary Player (III.307) 54
The Song of One Come to Confusion (NP, 157) 29
"The streams of time" (II.275) 16
"Suppose I make a timepiece of humanity" (III.295) 55

The Tables of Destiny, Excerpt from (M.III.467) 169
The Tangled Wood (II.34) 22
"These tenuous Japanese shadows" (II.205) 30
"They used to have a cow" (V.78) 46
"Today Mount Mashuk is a hound dog" (III.187) 51
To the Artists of the World (V.216) 146
The Trumpet of the Martians (V.151) 126

"Unbending as a Boris Godunov boyarina" (II.238) 36
Usa-Gali (IV.37) 76

"Water eats at the rippling" (III.106) 29
"We chant and enchant" (II.42) 20
"When horses die, they sigh" (II.97) 28
"When I was young I went alone" (III, 306) 34
"Where the winking waxwings whistle" (II.276) 16
"Who wants to hear a story" (II.39) 21
"Wind whose" (II.258) 29
The Word as Such (V.247) 119
The World in Reverse (IV.239) 68

"The year the girls first called me 'gramps' " (V.72) 52
"You are my song, my dark blue dream" (II.277) 17

Zangezi (III.315) 191

The King of Time is set in Linotron Galliard, a typeface designed by Matthew Carter and issued by the Mergenthaler Linotype Company in 1978. Basing his work on an original design cut by Robert Granjon in 1570, Carter created for photocomposition a new face with a variety of weights and swash characters; it has a flair that seems appropriate to Khlebnikov.

Design: Copenhaver Cumpston
Composition: NK Graphics
Printing: The Vail-Ballou Press